THE ULTI
GUIDE TO UK MOTORCYCLING: GET YOUR LICENCE AND RIDE

BY GOKHAN DARCAN

Publisher's note

All information contained in this book is based on personal knowledge, experience and research. Whilst every good faith effort has been made to ensure accuracy, some details may be inaccurate, become obsolete or out of date. Use of the information contained in this book is at your own risk. The Author and Publisher cannot be held responsible for any legal or personal problems arising from the use of this information.

You are strongly advised to always consult official UK government sources for up-to-date, official advice and details, or seek professional advice where necessary. This book is intended as a practical, supplementary guide, official sources should always be your go-to source for the most accurate and up-to-date legal and regulatory information.

ISBN: 978-1-0683258-3-0

DRCN Publishing
www.darcan.net/books

First published: December 2024

Book Cover Design, Graphics and Illustration designs (except road signs and CE label) and Cover Photograph taken in Snowdonia - Wales, were created by Gokhan Darcan.

TABLE OF CONTENTS

To my daughter,
May you always have the courage to chase your dreams and the freedom to forge your own path. This book is for you and all the journeys yet to come.

To my wife,
My unwavering supporter and greatest believer, thank you for standing by me, always.

To my mom,
For your endless encouragement, belief, and trust in me.

INTRODUCTION

Welcome to **The Ultimate Guide to UK Motorcycling: Get Your Licence and Ride**.

Contrary to what one might think of as rainy, gloomy and cold UK roads, the thrill of riding a motorcycle (sometimes called a 'motorbike' or 'bike') is truly priceless. However, there are many steps to take before you can enjoy this sense of freedom, from getting the right licence to understanding the various tests and legal requirements. I have designed **The Ultimate Guide to UK Motorcycling: Get Your Licence and Ride** to be the definitive guide to your journey, making the entire process clear, and accessible to everyone from beginners to experienced riders.

As the author, this is my first informative book and when I started my own motorcycling journey in the UK, I was faced with the confusion and uncertainty that a lot of the information was in pieces elsewhere, which led me to take action. As an experienced international rider, I have experienced the challenges of starting out in a new motorcycling environment.

One of my first observations in the UK was that the average age of motorcyclists was high. I then embarked on the UK licensing process and then tried to uncover the reasons for this through research and conversations. Although the young generation in the UK who have reached the age of motorcycling have a desire to ride a motorcycle, the confusion that begins with the complexity of the licensing process they encounter, and the fact that young people between the ages of 17-24 are pushed towards driving, emerges as one of the biggest reasons. As a result, I realised how difficult it is to find a comprehensive guide that covers everything needed to get a licence and ride safely in the UK. This is again one of the contributing reasons why young people in particular are not able to enter the world of motorcycling. Information is often scattered across multiple platforms, making it difficult for new riders to gather all the information they need.

Despite the numerous resources dedicated to cyclists, motorcyclists unfortunately face a lack of consolidated, practical advice. The steps to getting a motorcycle licence, understanding the various tests and mastering the practical aspects of riding are scattered, making it clearly difficult for new riders to know where to start. This book aims to fill this gap by providing a complete guide to the entire process.

WHY THIS BOOK IS NEEDED

Motorcycling is a cost effective form of transport and recreation in the UK, but clear guidance for new and experienced riders is fragmented. Many people find the process of getting a licence confusing, with different categories and tests required for each type of motorcycle licence. Beyond passing the tests, riders also face a lack of advice on basics such as practical riding skills, safety and regular motorcycle maintenance.

My aim with **The Ultimate Guide to UK Motorcycling: Get Your Licence and Ride** is to provide a single, reliable guide that simplifies the entire process. I aim to provide a comprehensive reference guide from understanding the differences between licence categories, to preparing for the tests, making sure your bike is roadworthy and connecting with the UK's vibrant motorcycling community. I have designed it not only to help new riders, but also to support those looking to upgrade their licence, improve their riding skills or dive deeper into the world of motorcycling.

A WORD OF CAUTION

While this book is designed to provide helpful guidance and insight into the process of obtaining a motorcycle licence and becoming a skilled rider, it is important to note that it is not an official guide. All information contained in this book is based on my personal experience and research and whilst every effort has been made to ensure accuracy, some details may become out of date over time. I cannot be held responsible for any legal or personal issues arising from the use of this information.

For up-to-date, official advice and details, I strongly recommend that you always consult official UK government sources or seek professional advice where necessary. This book is intended as a practical, supplementary guide, official sources should always be your go-to source for the most accurate and up-to-date legal and regulatory information.

HOW TO USE THIS BOOK

Although I have designed the flow of the book to put the information and needs on top of each chapter in each chapter, I tried to design every chapter as a guide to enable you to reach your needs quickly by going directly to the subject you want alone. For this reason, you can read the chapters in order or out of order.

If you do not have a smartphone, instead of scanning QR code, you can access the required document or website link by visiting **www.darcan.net/links** and entering the **Code** under the barcode.

For example, if you cannot scan the QR code on the side with your smartphone or another QR code reader, you can enter the code below the QR code **c48d23** at the web address I shared.

Code: c48d23

WHAT YOU'LL LEARN

This book covers the whole spectrum of motorcycling in the UK, from getting your first licence to developing advanced skills. Here are some of the key topics you'll find inside:

Types of UK Motorcycle Licences: Whether you're aiming to get a moped licence at 16 or working your way up to an unrestricted Category A licence, this book will explain each step and requirement in clear terms. I explain the different routes you can take, the relevant age restrictions and the stages of progression from one category to the next.

Compulsory Basic Training (CBT): If you're new to riding, CBT is your first step. I explain what to expect during training, why it's necessary and how it prepares you for real-world riding.

Motorcycle Theory Test: This book aims to provide in-depth guidance on preparing for both sections of the theory test – the multiple choice questions and the hazard perception test. I share essential study tips and the key topics to focus on so you can pass with confidence.

Practical Tests (Mod 1 and Mod 2): Passing the practical tests is often the most difficult part of getting your motorcycle licence. Here, I go into detail about each test, explaining the specific manoeuvres and skills assessed and giving practical advice to help you succeed.

Legal and Maintenance Requirements: Being a responsible motorcyclist goes beyond passing your tests. You also need to keep your motorcycle in good condition and comply with UK laws. This book tries to cover everything you need to know to stay safe and legal on the road, including regular servicing, MOT requirements, insurance and tax checklists and everything else you need to know to stay safe and legal on the road.

Motorcycle Safety and Riding Etiquette: Safety is paramount when riding a motorcycle. I cover the essentials, including defensive riding, correct road positioning and riding techniques in adverse weather conditions. I also cover riding in groups, communicating with other riders and developing habits that will keep you safe.

Advanced Riding Skills and Training: Once you've passed the basic tests, there's more to learn. From advanced riding courses with organisations such as IAM RoadSmart and RoSPA to off-road riding skills and track days, this book offers guidance on how to become a more skilled and confident rider.

UK Motorcycle Community: Motorcycling is not just about getting from A to B; it's about joining a community. This book introduces you to motorcycle clubs, social groups and online forums where you can connect with other riders, attend events and become part of the UK's vibrant motorcycle culture.

Many More Topics: Apart from the topics I mentioned above, you can find the mistakes made by beginner motorcycle riders, how to correct them, how to ensure the safety of your motorcycle, how to prepare for short and long motorcycle tours and many other useful topics in the book.

A RESOURCE FOR ALL RIDERS

Whether you're just starting out or looking to improve your riding skills, **The Ultimate Guide to UK Motorcycling: Get Your Licence and Ride** is a guide for every stage of your motorcycling journey. My aim is to provide a comprehensive and accessible resource to help you through the process of becoming a licensed rider and beyond. I want you to feel empowered, confident and excited about the world of motorcycling in the UK.

This book is a response to the need for clear, consolidated information in the motorcycling world; a resource that simplifies the often confusing maze of tests, regulations and riding skills. Motorcyclists are not alone with this book. By bringing almost everything together in one practical guide, I hope to bridge the gap and make it easier for new and experienced riders to enjoy all the benefits and adventures that come with riding in the UK.

Let's get started on your journey to your UK motorcycling licence and a lifetime of riding!

1. TYPES OF MOTORCYCLE LICENCES

There are a number of different routes to a motorcycle licence in the UK, each allowing you to ride motorcycles with different engine sizes (cc) and power levels. These categories are designed to suit the experience and age of the rider, and have specific restrictions depending on the type of licence you are pursuing. Some routes have age restrictions, while others expand your options for riding more powerful motorcycles as you progress through the licensing stages.

First of all, it's important to understand a key term that you will come across on most licensing routes: **CBT** or **Compulsory Basic Training**. This is a fundamental step that you will need to complete before you can progress on your motorcycling journey in the UK.

If you passed your **car driving test before February 2001**, you are legally allowed to ride a moped up to 50cc without L-plates and carry a passenger as long as you do not exceed the 28mph speed limit. However, if you have little or no experience of riding, I strongly recommend that you take the Compulsory Basic Training (CBT) course to develop a solid understanding of motorcycling skills and safety.

In **Northern Ireland**, the rules are slightly different;

- If you passed your **car driving test before 21st February 2011**, you are allowed to ride a moped without L plates, but it is still recommended that you complete the CBT before you set off.

- If you passed your **car driving test after 21st February 2011**, you must complete a CBT course before riding moped on the road.

For everyone else, it is mandatory to complete a Compulsory Basic Training (CBT) course before you can ride a moped or motorcycle. A CBT is a day course that can be taken if you have a UK provisional driving licence, a full UK driving licence, or an EU driving licence registered with the DVLA. The minimum age requirement varies: **if you are 16 or over**, you can take a CBT to ride a moped up to 50cc.

If you have completed your CBT and do not have a full car licence:

- You must display your L-plates when riding.
- You cannot carry passengers.
- You are not allowed to ride on motorways.

If you have completed your CBT and have a full car licence:

- You are not allowed to ride on motorways.
- You do not need to renew your CBT to ride mopeds.
- You can ride mopeds until your car licence expires.

From the age of 17, after successfully completing your CBT, you are entitled to ride a motorcycle or scooter up to 125cc for a period of two years. However, during this time:

- You must display your L-plates.
- You cannot carry passengers.
- You are not allowed to ride on motorways.

A CBT is normally valid for two years. Once your CBT has expired, you will need to retake the course and move on to further tests if you want to progress towards a full motorcycle licence. You can find all the details about the CBT in **Chapter 2**.

It is also worth noting that, like the CBT, the Theory Test has also an expiry date. Once you have passed the Theory Test, you will also have two years to complete your practical tests before your Theory Test result expires.

Here is a list of the Licences and I will cover their details on the following pages:

1. **AM Moped Licence (with CBT only)**

2. **AM Moped Licence (with theory and practical tests)**

3. **A1 Light Motorcycle Licence (maximum power 11kW)**

4. **A2 Restricted Motorcycle Licence (maximum power 35kW)**

5. **Full Unrestricted Category A Licence (Direct Access Scheme)**

1.1 AM MOPED LICENCE (WITH CBT ONLY)

If you are 16 years old and have a provisional licence, you can start your journey into moped riding by completing Compulsory Basic Training (CBT). However, you are allowed to ride any moped or scooter with an engine capacity of up to 50cc, as long as it is restricted to a top speed of 28mph (45km/h). However, there are a few restrictions:

- You must display L-plates (Learner plates) on your vehicle.
- You are not allowed to carry passengers.
- Riding on motorways is prohibited.
- This provisional entitlement lasts for two years, after which you will need to either renew the CBT and take further tests to progress to a full moped or motorcycle licence.

1.2 AM MOPED LICENCE (WITH THEORY AND PRACTICAL TESTS)

To convert a provisional AM licence into a permanent one, you must pass both a theory and practical test.

- **Eligibility**: The minimum age requirement is 16.
- **Steps**: After completing CBT, you must pass the **Motorcycle Theory Test** and **Practical Test** on a 50cc moped.

- **Entitlements:** Once you have successfully passed both tests, you can ride a 50cc moped without needing L-plates. You can also:
    - Carry a passenger. (Remember to add the passenger-pillion cover to your insurance)
    - Due to the speed restrictions on mopeds, riding on motorways is prohibited. This is because you need to exceed 30mph to ride safely on motorways, which is not possible on a moped, which is a speed restricted vehicle.

On the next page you can find the AM Moped Path Route Diagram.

AM Moped Path

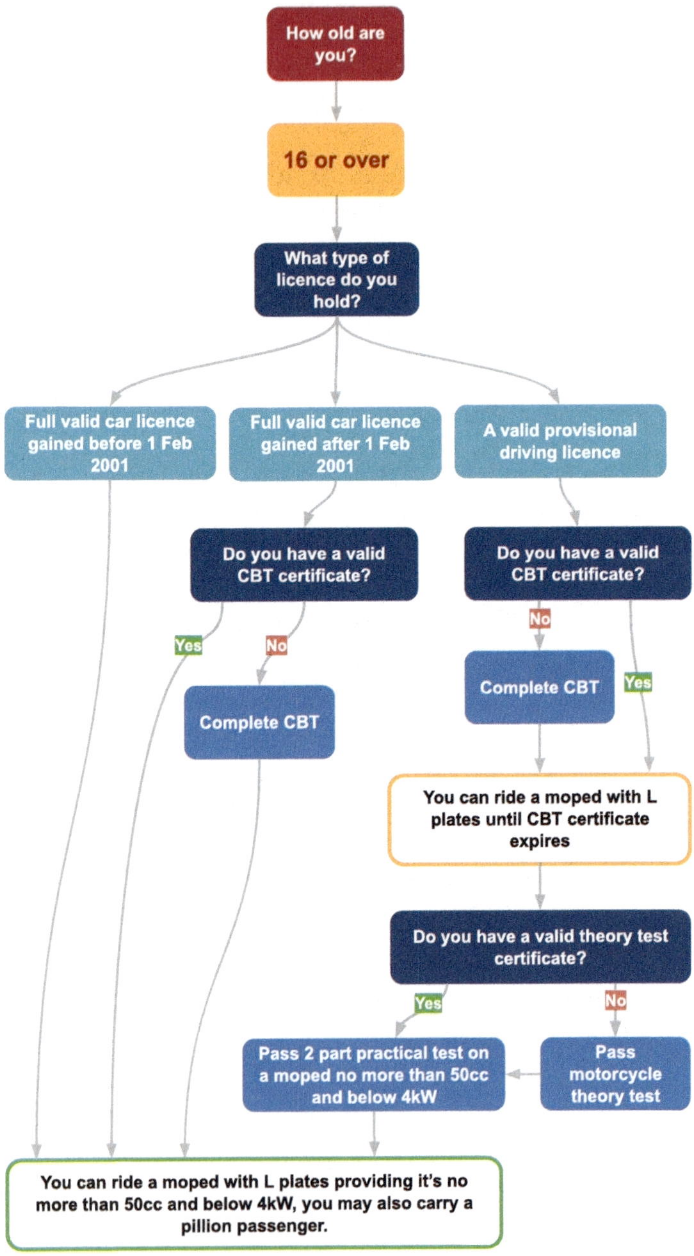

1.3 A1 LIGHT MOTORCYCLE LICENCE (MAXIMUM POWER 11KW)

If you are 17 or over, you can aim for the A1 light motorcycle licence, which gives you more flexibility and the ability to ride slightly more powerful machines.

- **Eligibility:** The minimum age requirement is 17.
- **Steps:** Once you have completed the CBT, you must pass the **Motorcycle Theory Test** and **Practical Test** on a motorcycle with an engine capacity between 120cc and 125cc.
- **Entitlements:** Once you have completed both tests, you are entitled to:
    - Ride motorcycles up to 125cc with a maximum power output of 11kW (approximately 14.8 horsepower).
    - You no longer required to display L-plates.
    - You are allowed to carry passengers. (Remember to add passenger-pillion protection to your insurance)
    - You can ride on motorways.
- **Upgrade Opportunity:** After holding an A1 licence for at least two years, you can move on to an **A2 licence** with a more advanced practical exam, opening the doors to even more powerful motorcycles.

On the next page you can find the A1 light motorcycle Path Route Diagram.

A1 light motorcycle path

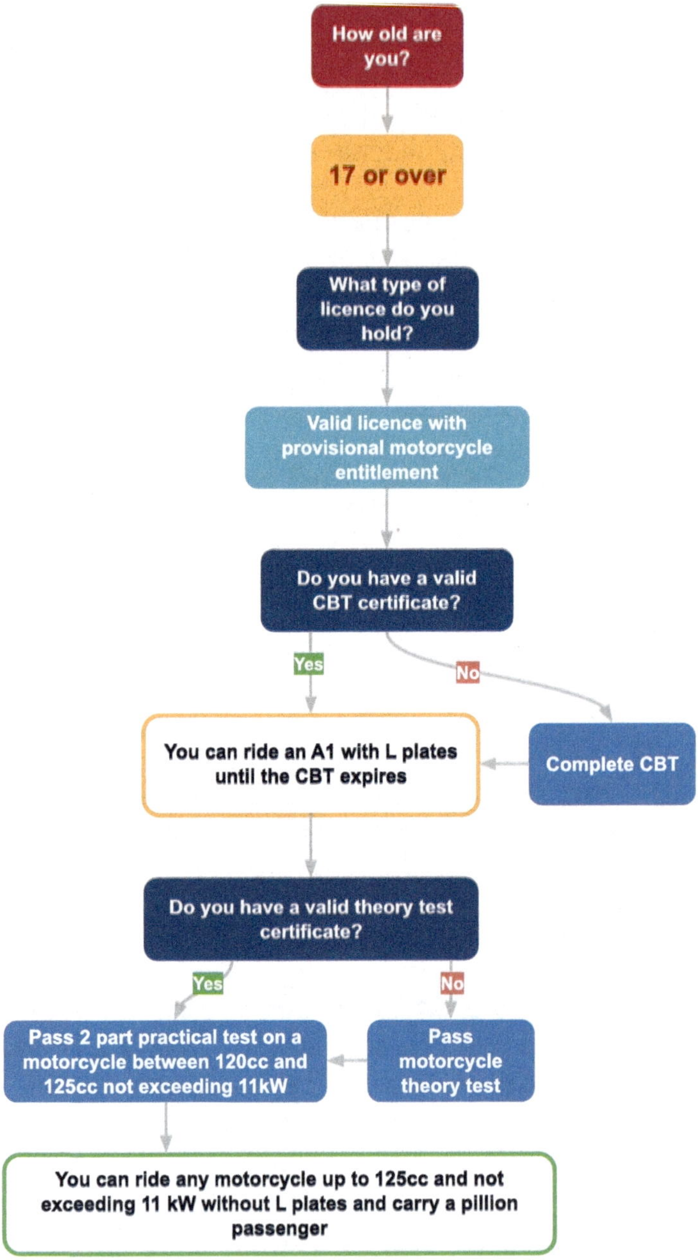

1.4 A2 RESTRICTED MOTORCYCLE LICENCE (MAXIMUM POWER 35KW)

If you are 19 or over and want to ride more powerful motorcycles, then the A2 restricted licence is the next step.

- **Eligibility:** The minimum age requirement is 19.
- **Steps:** As with other categories, you will need to complete the **CBT**, pass the **Motorcycle Theory Test** and then pass the **Practical Test** on a motorcycle with an engine capacity exceeding 395cc and a power output between 25kW and 35kW (approximately 33 to 47 horsepower).
- **Entitlements:** With an A2 licence you can:
    - Ride motorcycles with a power output of up to 35kW.
    - You are allowed to carry passengers. (Remember to add passenger-pillion protection to your insurance)
    - You can ride on motorways without restrictions.
- **Upgrade Opportunity:** After two years with an A2 licence, you can take a further practical test and move on to a fully unrestricted **Category A** licence, allowing you to ride any motorcycle without any power restrictions.

On the next page you can find the A2 Motorcycle Path Route Diagram.

A2 motorcycle path

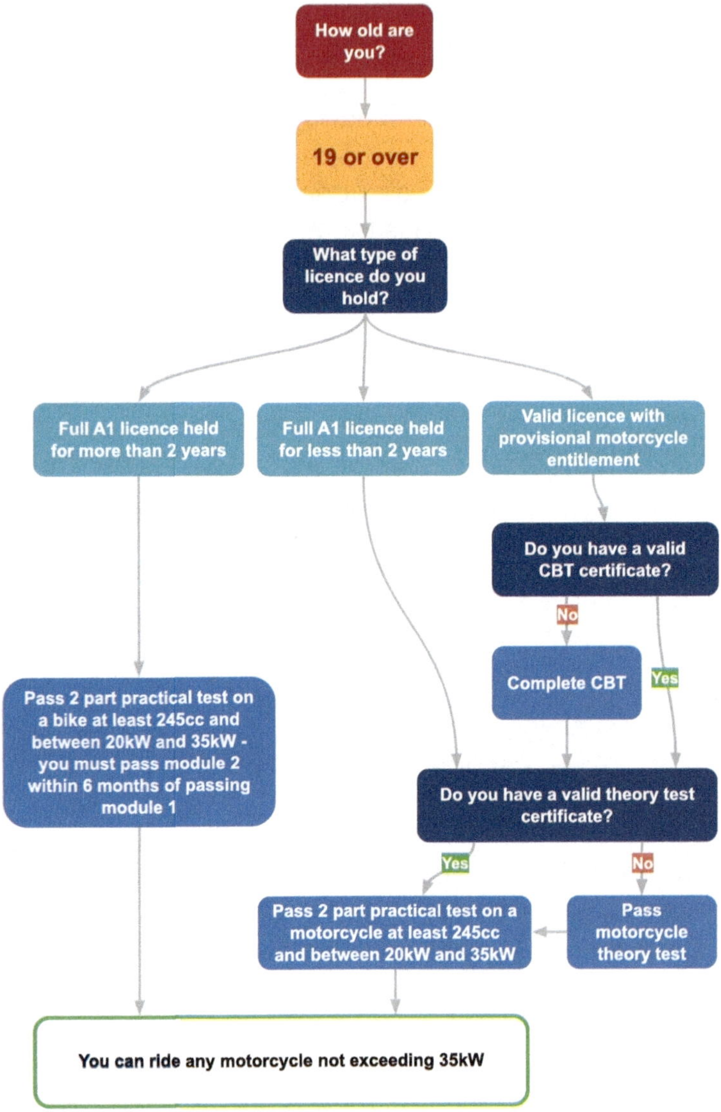

1.5 FULL UNRESTRICTED CATEGORY 'A' LICENCE (DAS: DIRECT ACCESS SCHEME)

A fully unrestricted Category A licence allows you to ride any motorcycle, regardless of engine size or power output, and is the ultimate goal for many riders.

- **Eligibility:** The minimum age requirement is 24, but you can also access it at 21 if you've held an A2 licence for at least two years.

- **Steps:** As with other categories, you must complete the **CBT**, pass the **Motorcycle Theory Test** and then pass the **Practical Test** on a motorcycle with a minimum power output of 35kW.

- **Entitlements:** Once you've obtained a Category A licence, you can:

    - Ride any motorcycle, regardless of size or power.

    - You are allowed to carry passengers. (Remember to add passenger-pillion protection to your insurance)

    - Ride on motorways.

- **Direct Access vs Progressive Access:** If you're aged 24 or over and don't want to progress to a staged progressing, you can get a **Direct Access Scheme (DAS)** which allows you to apply directly for a full Category A licence once you've completed the necessary tests.

You can find the Category A motorcycle Path Route Diagrams for the age between 21 to 23 and 24 or over on the next pages.

Category A motorcycle (21 to 23) path

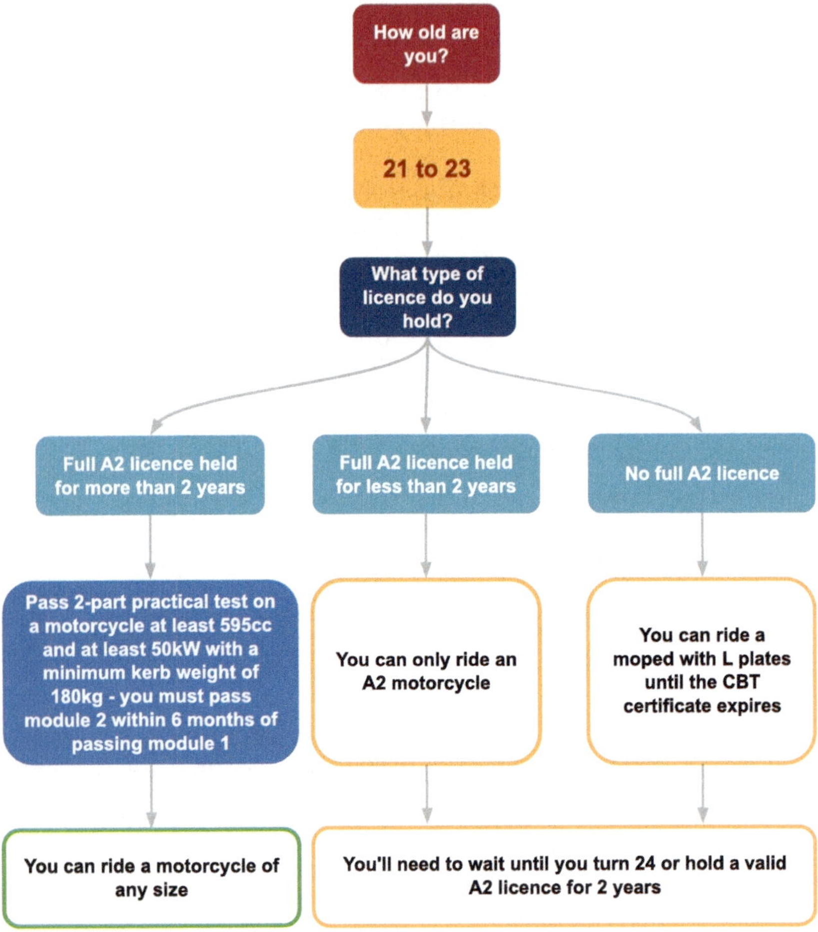

Category A motorcycle (24 or over) path

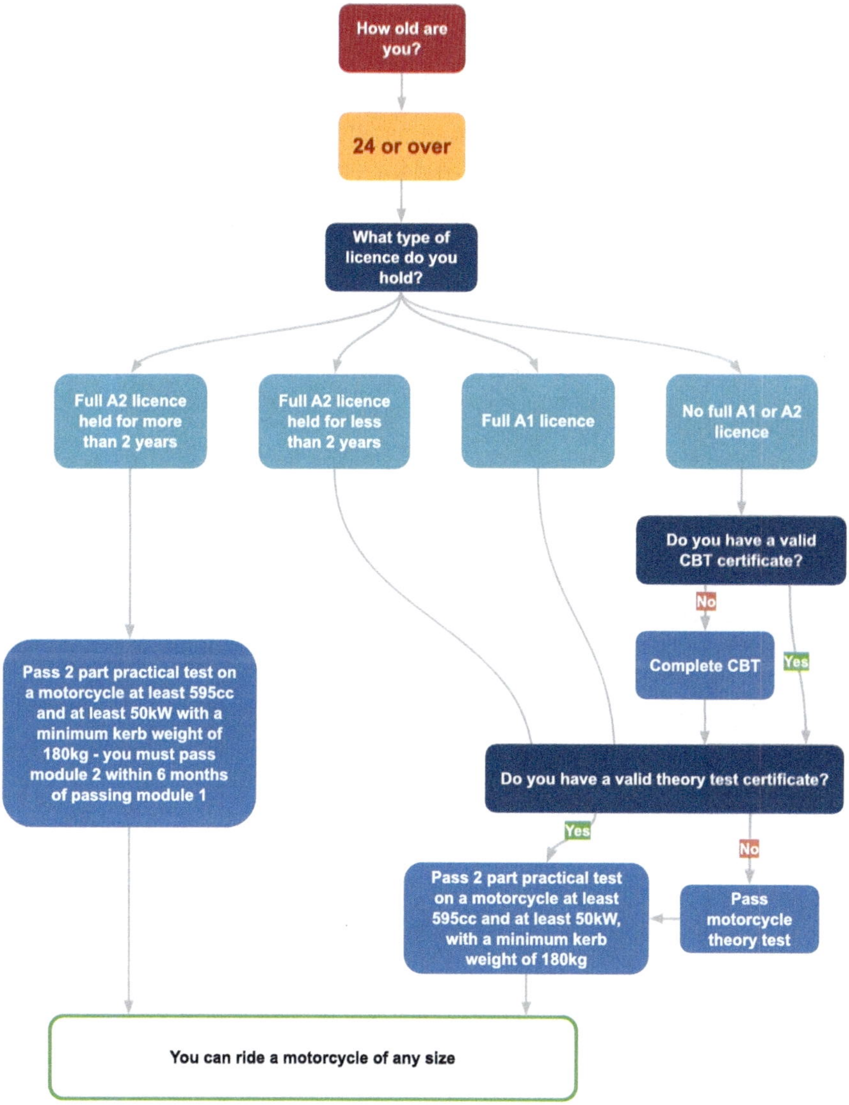

In this chapter, I have covered the gradual steps from riding a basic moped at the age of 16 to riding an unrestricted motorcycle at the age of 24, as well as information about direct access scheme after the age 24.

With the details here, I have compiled information that will help you become more familiar with all motorcycle licence processes and make it easier for you to choose the path that suits you and move forward.

2. COMPULSORY BASIC TRAINING (CBT)

Anyone wishing to ride a moped, scooter, or motorcycle in the UK must complete Compulsory Basic Training (CBT). This one-day training is intended to give you the skills and knowledge you need to ride safely on the road, regardless of whether you're a total novice or are getting back into riding after a long break. The CBT is not a test in the traditional sense, but a course that must be successfully completed before you can legally ride on UK roads with a provisional licence.

In this chapter, I will share the structure of the CBT, what to expect on the day and the key elements that will prepare you for safe, confident riding.

What is CBT?

The CBT is compulsory for anyone wishing to ride a moped scooter or motorcycle on UK roads, except those who passed their driving test before February 2001. Introduced in 1990, the CBT was designed to improve road safety for motorcyclists by providing a basic level of proficiency before riding on public roads and to reduce accidents involving inexperienced riders.

The rules are slightly different in **Northern Ireland**. If you passed your driving test before 21 February 2011, you are eligible to ride a moped without L-plates, but for your own safety, I would recommend that you complete the CBT before you set off if you have no previous experience.

However, if you passed your driving test after this date, you must complete a CBT course before you can ride a moped on the road.

Once the CBT has been completed, riders can ride:

- Mopeds (up to 50cc) at age 16.
- Motorcycles and scooters up to 125cc (maximum power of 11kW) at age 17.

However, riders must still display L-plates (L or D plates in Wales), cannot carry passengers and are not allowed on motorways. This certificate is valid for two years, after which a CBT must be taken again unless the rider has switched to a full motorcycle licence.

For full car driving licence holders:

There is a slight difference when it comes to mopeds. If you are a driver with any full car licence who has completed a CBT, you do not need to display L-plates and can carry passengers. If you were licensed before February 2001 then you do not need to display L-plates and can carry passengers, even if you do not have a CBT.

Structure of the CBT

The CBT course is divided into five key sections. Each section builds on the previous one, aiming to leave you with a clear understanding of how to control your motorcycle or moped and how to ride safely on public roads at the end of the day. The five sections are:

1. **Introduction and Eye Test**
2. **Practical On-Site Training**
3. **Practical On-Site Riding**
4. **Practical On-Road Training**
5. **Practical On-Road Riding**

Each section will be completed at your own pace and your instructor will not allow you to move on to the next section until you are confident in your abilities.

2.1 INTRODUCTION AND EYE TEST

The day starts with an introduction to CBT where your instructor will explain the purpose of the course and what you will be doing during the day. This includes safety briefings and the legal requirements for riding on UK roads. You will be informed that you will need appropriate protective clothing including helmets, gloves, jackets and suitable footwear. Generally, CBT courses will provide a loaner helmet if you do not have your own helmet with you, however, if you do not have boots or shoes that are high enough to protect your ankles, they may not accept you on the course.

You will also have a basic **eye test** to ensure that your vision meets the legal requirements for riding. This is usually considered sufficient to read a number plate from a distance of 20 metres (or 20.5 metres for older plates). If you need glasses or contact lenses to meet this requirement, you should wear them throughout the course.

While in some countries the use of glasses or contact lenses is recorded on driving licences, in the UK there is no such statement on driving licences. However, it is mandatory that you drive/ride in a way that allows you to read the number plate from the distance I have specified above.

2.2 PRACTICAL ON-SITE TRAINING

The second part of the day involves getting to know the motorcycle or moped you will be riding. This is done in a controlled, off-road environment, usually a car park or a special training area.

Your instructor will explain the basic mechanics of the vehicle, including:

- **Understanding the controls:** The throttle, brakes, gears (for manual bikes), indicators, horn and how to start and stop the engine.
- **Braking and throttle control:** How to use the front and rear brakes correctly and adjust the throttle.
- **Steering and balancing:** Tips on maintaining balance and steering properly, especially at lower speeds.
- The importance of **motorcycle checks** before riding, such as tyre pressure, lights, and brakes.

This session is essential to build your confidence in the motorcycle before you start riding and to understand how it works.

2.3 PRACTICAL ON-SITE RIDING

Once you have become comfortable with a motorcycle, scooter or moped in the previous section, you will move on to practice your riding skills in the same controlled environment. This section covers the basic skills required for safe road use.

Some of the basic exercises in this section are:

- **Moving off and stopping:** How to start smoothly from a stationary position and stop in a controlled manner.
- **Low-speed manoeuvres:** You will practice riding in a straight line at low speed, as well as making U-turns and going around obstacles to build balance and control.
- **Gear changes:** If you're on a manual motorcycle, you'll learn how to shift gears properly without stalling or jerking the bike.
- **Emergency stops:** Practicing a sudden stop to avoid hazards in a controlled manner.
- **Turning and cornering:** Learning how to lean into turns safely and position yourself correctly in bends.

You'll practice these manoeuvres until your instructor feels you are confident enough to move on to the next stage.

2.4 PRACTICAL ON-ROAD TRAINING

Before you hit the public roads, you will receive classroom-style training focusing on road riding theory with the skills you learn on-site. In this short training, you will learn about road safety, awareness and the legal requirements for motorcyclists. If you already have a basic understanding of the **Highway Code**, this will help you make the most of this relatively short training session.

Some of the following topics in this section are:

- **The Highway Code:** Being familiar with traffic rules the road, including signs, signals and road markings.
- **Road positioning:** How to safely and visibly position yourself on the road to other road users.
- **Hazard awareness:** Developing to spot potential hazards early and how to react appropriately.
- **Legal requirements:** Making sure you understand the law regarding riding with L-plates, wearing protective equipment and insurance.

Your instructor will also prepare you for the next Practical On-Road Ride by talking about the types of roads you will be riding on and specific scenarios you may encounter, such as roundabouts, junctions and pedestrian crossings.

2.5 PRACTICAL ON-ROAD RIDING

The final and most important part of the CBT is the riding on the public road section. You will usually have a practical on-road riding session with the instructor via a one-way radio to give you real-time instructions and feedback.

In this session you will be expected to demonstrate all the skills you have learned throughout the day, some of them are:

- **Moving off and stopping:** How to safely start from a stationary position and stop at junctions and traffic lights.
- **Road positioning:** Maintaining the correct position on the road, especially when riding in traffic or on busy roads.

- **Observations:** Demonstrating the use of mirrors and shoulder checks (life savers) before changing direction or speed.
- **Signalling:** Using your signals correctly and in good time before turns, lane changes and roundabouts, and switching them off when the turn is over.
- **General road awareness:** Showing your response appropriately to traffic conditions, pedestrians and other road users throughout the ride.

The road riding section of the CBT will usually be attended by an instructor with one or two students. It usually takes around two hours, depending on your progress, either one-to-one or with another student. Your instructor will assess your ability to ride safely and confidently on different road conditions, including quiet residential streets and busier roads.

2.6 TIPS FOR A SUCCESSFUL CBT

- **Wear proper gear:** While a helmet and visor/goggles are mandatory for motorcycling on the road in the UK, it is always a wise choice to wear full protective equipment including gloves, boots and a motorcycle jacket, even if this is not legally required for CBT.
- **Stay relaxed:** It is perfectly normal to feel nervous at times in these environments, but as long as you try to stay calm and listen carefully to your instructor's feedback, you will be fine. Instructors are there to help you, not to judge you.
- **Practice makes perfect:** It may be your first time on a motorcycle and you are struggling with any part of the training, never hesitate to ask for more time to

practice. You can always come back for additional lessons if necessary, and with more practice you can reach your goal.

- **Focus on safety:** Never forget that safe riding is the ultimate goal. Take your time and attention to learn and understand the safety principles and don't rush the process.

What Happens Next?

Once you have completed all five parts of the CBT, your instructor will give you a **DL196 certificate** to prove that you have successfully completed the course. This certificate allows you to legally ride on UK roads (except motorways) with a provisional licence, unlike the licences we covered in **Chapter 1**.

However, it is important to remember that the CBT is only valid for two years. During this time, you can move on to your full motorcycle licence exams (such as AM, A1, A2 or A licences), which I will cover in later chapters. If you do not take or pass your full motorcycle exams, you will need to complete the CBT again.

Why CBT is Important

It would not be wrong to say that it is an important step in creating road safety for other road users when new riders take to the public roads, as well as being a mandatory requirement for new riders.

While some people may see CBT as a simple box-ticking exercise, it is also a very valuable step in practice as it opens your horizons to developing important riding skills, the importance of observation and road awareness, and gives you the opportunity to practice using your motorcycle, scooter or moped in real life situations.

After you've completed your CBT, you'll be prepared to put everything you've learnt into practice on the road and have fun doing it.

In this chapter, I have attempted to provide a comprehensive overview of the CBT process, which is the first step towards becoming a fully licensed motorcyclist in the UK. In the next section I will cover the theory test, which is a requirement for progressing through the various licensing categories.

3. MOTORCYCLE THEORY TEST

The way to progress towards a full motorcycle licence in the UK is to pass the theory test alongside the CBT. In this chapter I will try to help you understand the importance of being an efficient, safe and knowledgeable rider for the theory test, with direct access to important resources.

3.1 WHAT IS THE MOTORCYCLE THEORY TEST?

The motorcycle theory test is designed to assess your knowledge of the general and UK rules of the road, hazard information and motorcycle specific safety criteria.

It consists of two parts:

- **Multiple-choice questions:** This will focus on the Highway Code, road hazards and motorcycle specific regulations.

- **Hazard perception test:** Tests your ability to identify and react to potential hazards while riding.

You will need to pass both parts of the test, which are taken at the same time frame of the test, to be eligible to take your practical tests (Mod 1 and Mod 2).

3.2 WHO NEEDS TO TAKE THE MOTORCYCLE THEORY TEST?

You will usually need to pass a motorcycle theory test before you can move on to your practical motorcycle tests. This step is essential for most riders on their journey to a full motorcycle licence.

There are a few exceptions to this, however:

- If you have passed a moped test after 1 July 1996, you will not need to take a motorcycle theory test if:
    - You are taking a Category A1 (small motorcycle) licence; or
    - You are upgrading your motorcycle licence under the 'progressive access' (also known as 'staged access') rules.

If You Hold a Car Licence

Even if you already have a car licence, you will still need to pass a motorcycle theory test before you can take any practical motorcycle tests. This is a separate requirement specific to motorcycles and will ensure that you are well prepared for the unique challenges of riding.

You should make sure that you check which motorcycles you can ride and which tests you will need to take to gain the category of licence you want. I have detailed the roadmaps for this in **Chapter 1**.

3.3 PREPARING FOR THE MULTIPLE-CHOICE TEST

3.3.1 STRUCTURE OF THE TEST

The multiple choice section of the theory test consists of **50 questions** in total, of which you must answer **43 questions correctly** (an 86% pass mark is required). The questions are based on the following main topics:

- **The Highway Code:** Topics mainly in the highway code includes general road rules and legal requirements.
- **Motorcycle Specific Questions:** Topics such as motorcycle maintenance, road positioning and safety equipment.
- **Road Signs and Signals:** Understanding the signs and signals required for safe riding.

You will have **57 minutes** to complete the test and it will be done on a computer at an official test centre.

I recommend that you do not bring much with you to the test, as in test centres, your wristwatch and even your coat will not be allowed into the test cabin. You will usually be provided with small lockers for these items.

3.3.2 STUDY RESOURCES

- **The Official DVSA Theory Test Kit:** The official resource from DVSA (Driver and Vehicle Standards Agency), you can get all the information and practice questions you need in book and

Code: eb4a90

smartphone app format. You can access the details of the official resource by scanning the QR code.

Code: 45693b

• **Online Practice Tests:** Many websites offer free tests that are close to the real one, and you can easily find them by searching the web. It is easy to find with search like "motorcycle theory test practice". These websites and smartphone apps will help you practice on a variety of practice questions, hazard perception simulations.

Code: 9c3564

• **The Highway Code:** You need to know the UK road rules inside and out. The Highway Code is available to read online for free or you can buy as a physical book. Scan the QR code on the side to get the official Highway Code online version.

3.3.3 KEY TOPICS TO FOCUS ON

There are areas of the multiple choice test where you may make mistakes, especially in areas that contain numerical information and are similar to each other, so I recommend that you prepare a little more carefully, especially in the following areas:

- **Speed Limits for Motorcycles:** Be familiar with the speed limits for motorcycles on different types of roads and try not to confuse them.
- **Overtaking Rules:** This is sometimes tricky part and be familiar with when it is legal and safe to overtake, including passing through traffic.

- **Motorcycle Maintenance:** Learn basic maintenance checks (such as tyres, brakes and lights) and what to do in the event of mechanical problems, or refresh your knowledge by going over what you already know.

- **Legal Responsibilities:** Be familiar with the legal requirements for tax, MOT, insurance and documentation.

- **Traffic Signs:** Be familiar with motorcyclist-specific signs, including restrictions, lane markings and warning signs.

3.4 THE HAZARD PERCEPTION TEST

3.4.1 STRUCTURE OF THE TEST

The hazard perception test consists of **14 video clips**, usually of real-life, sometimes computer-aided road scenes, and one of them, unlike the others, contains not one but two hazards. You must identify potential hazards as they develop and click the mouse when you see them. The maximum score per hazard is **5 points**, and you need to score at least **44 out of 75** to pass.

3.4.2 WHAT IS A HAZARD?

It would not be wrong to say that hazard has a definition that is based on events you observe in real life. Anything that can slow you down, stop you or change direction is a hazard. The test focuses to evaluate whether you can recognise changing and **developing dangerous situations** that require you to take action. We can list the examples of hazards as follows:

- **Vehicles changing lanes suddenly.**
- **Pedestrians stepping into the road.**
- **Cars pulling out from junctions.**
- **Roadworks or debris on the road.**

3.4.3 HOW TO SCORE WELL

- **Respond early:** The sooner you react and click when you notice a developing hazard, the more points you will get.
- **Avoid excessive clicking:** If you try to notice early and click too much in a short period of time, you may get zero points for that clip. Therefore, try to answer as carefully as possible and with fewer clicks when you are sure.
- **Practice:** In order to get used to the test format, there are many free and paid applications, especially in Smartphone application stores, that will help you develop your danger detection skills. In addition, some websites have interactive online features on these topics. You can find more alternatives to these tools by searching both in application stores and online.

3.5 TIPS FOR SUCCESS

Even if you have passed the car theory test before, you still need to be prepared and focused to pass the motorcycle theory test. Here are some tips to help you succeed:

3.5.1 DEVELOP A STUDY PLAN

Do not leave studying to the last minute, especially if you think you will forget the information for a long time, spend regular time studying the Highway Code, taking frequent practice tests and reviewing the basics. A well-structured study plan will ensure that you cover everything comprehensively and help you pass the test successfully.

3.5.2 TAKE PLENTY OF PRACTICE TESTS

As I mentioned in the previous section (Section 3.3.2), there are numerous practice tests available online and through smartphone apps. The more you practice, the more you will understand the types of questions asked and the format of the test.

3.5.3 LEARN FROM YOUR MISTAKES

Review your answers carefully during practice. Identify the areas where you tend to make mistakes and try to solve more practice tests to strengthen your understanding in these areas. As you gain more practice in areas where you think you have low confidence, you will find that you are getting stronger in those areas.

3.5.4 USE OFFICIAL RESOURCES

Try to use official DVSA resources as much as possible. These materials are designed to closely mirror the real test and are the main and most accurate reference sources to ensure that you have covered the relevant information.

3.5.5 STAY CALM ON TEST DAY

Try to stay calm and focused when you go into your theory test and if you are taking the test early in the morning, make sure you have had enough sleep the day before so that you do not have difficulty concentrating. You will have plenty of time to read each question carefully, use the full 57 minutes if necessary and do not rush.

You can mark any questions you are unsure of during the test and have the chance to go back and review them before you finish the test. This will help you to avoid wasting too much time on questions you are unsure of and to focus on them in the remaining time after all the questions have been completed.

3.6 AFTER PASSING THE THEORY TEST

When you reach this stage, you have taken an important step towards obtaining your full motorcycle license and you are one step closer to your goal. After this, you need to understand the next steps you need to complete and take action towards obtaining your full licence within the next two years and make the necessary preparations.

- **Certificate Validity:** Your theory test certificate is valid for two years, same as your CBT certificate. This means you have two years to complete both Module 1 and Module 2 of the practical riding tests to qualify for a full motorcycle licence.

- **Module 1 and Module 2 Practical Tests:**

    - **Module 1 (Mod 1):** This module is a clearly defined off the road test where you will demonstrate specific movements and skills in a specific pattern and not on a public road, focusing on basic motorcycle control including manoeuvres such as slaloms, U-turns and emergency stops. You cannot progress to

Module 2 without successfully completing Module 1.

- **Module 2 (Mod 2):** This is the on-road section where you will demonstrate your skills such as riding safely in real traffic conditions, navigating roundabouts and responding to hazards.

- **Booking Practical Tests:** Once your theory exam is complete, it is also worthwhile to carefully plan and schedule your Module 1 and Module 2 tests. Availability can vary depending on location and time of year, and popular test centres can have long waiting times, so planning early will ensure you have time to practice and book your test locations within the two-year validity period.

- **Preparation and Training:** Before taking Module 1 and Module 2, even if you are confident, I strongly recommend taking refresher lessons or practice rides. This will give you an advantage in terms of adaptation, especially even if you are an experienced rider in another country. Riding schools usually offer special packages for training after the theory test, which allows you to develop your skills, fine-tune areas that need improvement and get some tips from experienced instructors.

- **If You Don't Pass:** If for any reason you're unable to pass Module 1 and Module 2 practical tests within two years, your theory certificate will expire. This means you will need to retake the theory test to continue with your practical tests, and depending on when your CBT certificate is due, it might also need to be renewed.

3.7 RETAKING THE THEORY TEST

As I mentioned earlier, the multiple choice or the hazard perception is tested in the same test but in two sections. If you cannot pass any of these sections, do not be discouraged. You are not alone here, many riders like you cannot pass the theory test on the first try for various reasons. The important thing here is to know what to expect when you are in such a situation and how to benefit from this experience again and reach the final success you want in the best way.

- **Wait Period:** You can retake the theory test after **3 working days**, this will give you time to review the material without any long delays and consolidate your understanding. This waiting time is the same for each subsequent retake, the DVSA's aim here is to give you time to improve in this process by giving you a mandatory waiting time.

- **Feedback from the DVSA:** You will receive written feedback immediately after each attempt, indicating the areas where you did not meet the passing criteria.

  This feedback will show you which categories you made mistakes in, especially in the multiple choice section, and you will see a summary of how many points you scored for each of the hazard perception clips.

You can find an example of DVSA's failed theory test feedback after the test on the next page.

In this example test result, even though hazard perception was successful, the test was failed because the multiple-choice section was unsuccessful. You need to pass both sections at the same time.

Failed Theory Test Result Example:

I'm sorry to tell you that you've **failed** your **motorcycle** theory test.

Here are your scores

On the **multiple-choice** part, the pass mark is 43. You scored **41 out of 50**.

On the **hazard perception** part, the pass mark is 44. You scored **62 out of 75**.

You must pass both parts of the theory test to pass.

Here's the breakdown of your scores

Multiple-Choice	**Number of questions wrong**
Topic Area	
Safety Margins	2
Road and Traffic Signs	2
Other Types of Vehicle	1
Hazard Awareness	1
Alertness	1
Vehicle/Motorcycle Handling	2

Hazard Perception

On the double hazard you scored 8 points

You scored 5 points on 7 clips

You scored 4 points on 3 clips

You scored 3 points on 2 clips

You scored 1 point on 1 clip

- **Strategies for Improvement:**
    - **Review Weak Areas:** Using DVSA feedback, you can identify the subjects you scored lower on and focus your work on these subjects, helping you to make more effective use of your materials such as Highway Code and improve in these areas.
    - **Hazard Perception Practice:** If your hazard perception scores are low, it will be beneficial to increase the variety of video clips offered by many applications for hazard perception practice, solve more questions and better internalise hazard situations.
- **Additional Study Resources:**
    - **Riding Schools and Theory Workshops:** Some riding schools offer theory workshops or one-to-one sessions with instructors who specialise in test preparation. If you are having difficulty with this, you can get support from these schools and reinforce the subjects that are difficult for you with their guidance.
- **Building Confidence:** Although the DVSA allows you to book an appointment after 3 days from the failed test, don't rush into your next test until you feel fully prepared. Confidence comes from thorough preparation and while it's natural to be nervous, rushing can make you more nervous and will also mean that you'll incur additional financial costs each time you take the test.

Tips for Success:

- **Simulate Test Conditions:** If you find yourself running out of time on the actual test, try to mimic the real exam environment by taking uninterrupted time on your practice tests and timing yourself for each section. This technique will help improve your focus and reduce stress on test day.

- **Stay Positive and Patient:** It's perfectly normal to need more than one attempt to pass at times. Use each test as a stepping stone to build stronger knowledge and confidence.

Retaking your theory test can sometimes feel boring and challenging, but you can be sure that by using the feedback you receive effectively and focusing on your next attempt, you will be better equipped. When you put in the effort, each attempt will bring you closer to your goal of becoming a fully licensed rider.

Final Thought: Keep the Highway Code Handy

Even after you pass your theory test, the knowledge you gain will never lose its vital importance throughout your riding career. So, scanning the QR code on the side and having the official Highway Code document at hand will make you a safer rider as you gain more road experience and periodically review and reinforce the rules of the road.

Code: 9c3564

I have tried to give you a thorough overview of what to expect and what you will experience throughout the motorcycle theory test in this chapter. I will cover the practical tests you need take to advance to the different motorcycle licence categories in the next chapter.

4. PRACTICAL TESTS

Once you have completed your Compulsory Basic Training (CBT) and passed your theory test, the next step towards gaining your full motorcycle licence in the UK consists of two practical tests, taken separately but in order:

- **Module 1 (Mod 1)**
- **Module 2 (Mod 2)**

These tests will test your ability to ride a motorcycle, operate it safely and ride it competently on the road. You must successfully complete two practical tests, each with a distinct focus and format, in order to receive a full motorcycle licence.

Module 1 (Mod 1): This test will assess your ability to control your motorcycle through a series of off-road exercises conducted at a DVSA (Driver and Vehicle Standards Agency) test centre. It is intended to assess your fundamental motorcycle riding and handling abilities in an off-road setting utilising a controlled and pre-arranged system.

Module 2 (Mod 2): This test is a road riding test in which you will be observed by an examiner in a separate vehicle, usually a motorcycle but in some cases a car, behind you while riding in real traffic conditions. The examiner will assess your ability to ride safely in various road conditions and comply with the Highway Code while observing you from behind.

4.1 PREPARING FOR THE TESTS

Making sure you have enough practice before booking your Mod 1 or Mod 2 test will increase your chances of success in this part of test. Many riders attend formal training courses to prepare for both modules. This will not only increase your chances of passing the practical tests, but will also help you to be safer on the road and more comfortable during your tests.

Depending on the licence category you apply for, you can take your test on one of four types of motorcycle:

- **AM** (moped licence) – mopeds with an engine capacity of up to 50cc, with a top speed of 28mph.
- **A1** (light motorcycles) – scooters or motorcycles up to 125cc, with a maximum power output of 11kW.
- **A2** (medium motorcycles) – scooters or motorcycles with a maximum power output of 20-35kW.
- **A** (unrestricted motorcycles) – motorcycles with no power restrictions.

Practical tests are carried out on motorcycles that meet the requirements for the licence you are aiming to obtain, you cannot take the test for that class on a motorcycle from a different category.

4.2 MODULE 1 (MOD 1): OFF-ROAD MOTORCYCLE MANOEUVRES

Location: DVSA Test Centre (in a controlled off-road environment).

The Mod 1 test involves a number of motorcycle manoeuvres performed in a specific sequence designed to assess your control, balance and general handling ability. Keep in mind DVSA Test Centre doesn't supply any scooter or motorcycle. Mod 1 test takes approximately 15 to 20 minutes and includes the following exercises:

4.2.1 EXERCISES IN MOD 1

Manual handling:

This exercise tests your ability to safely handle your motorcycle from a standstill position. The examiner will ask you to walk alongside the motorcycle and push it manually before parking it in a clearly indicated spot. The purpose of this exercise is to show that, without of engine power, you have complete control over the motorcycle's weight and balance.

- **What to Expect:** You will need to be able to move your motorcycle forwards and backwards, usually in a parking area with lines or cones to show where to park.
- **Key Tips:**
    - Keep both hands firmly on the handlebars and maintain a good grip.
    - When reversing, gently apply the brake or brakes on the handlebars, which vary depending on

whether it is a motorcycle or a scooter, to control speed.

- Use your legs and body weight to manoeuvre the motorcycle into position, especially if you are parking in a tight space.

- At the end of the exercise, make sure the motorcycle is parked safely with the side stand or centre stand engaged before leaving the motorcycle alone.

Slalom and figure of 8:

This combination of exercises is to assess your ability to control the motorcycle with precision at low speeds. First, you'll slalom through a series of cones, turning quickly left and right. Once complete, you will perform a figure-of-eight manoeuvre, continuing to demonstrate your balance and throttle control.

- **What to Expect:** The examiner will take you through a series of cones arranged in a row. After the slalom, you will move into an open area to perform a figure-of-eight, which involves doing two smooth circles. Here, the cones will continue to be used in the figure eight, so make your turn accordingly.

- **Key Tips:**

  - **Throttle and clutch control** are critical here. Use the clutch to adjust your speed while keeping your revs steady, so you can use the clutch to accelerate and decelerate.

  - Slightly shift your body weight into each turn and keep your posture relaxed.

- Look where you want to go, especially during figure-of-eights, as looking at the cones will make you lose your balance.
- Keep your steering response smooth and avoid sudden movements to maintain balance.

Slow ride:

The slow ride exercise tests your ability to control the motorcycle at a very low speed by simulating situations such as riding in traffic or in congested areas. Although no line is used to measure the straightness of this slow ride, you will need to ride straight at walking pace without wobbling or losing your balance.

- **What to Expect:** Here the examiner will ask you to ride in a straight line at walking pace which generally the pace of examiner walking for approximately 10-15 meters while maintaining your balance without putting your feet on the ground.
- **Key Tips:**
    - To move the motorcycle at a slow speed, you can provide stability by gently applying the **rear brake** while holding the clutch in the friction area, that is, where the clutch partially engages.
    - To help maintain balance, look straight ahead, not at the motorcycle or the ground, as this will help you go more stable and straight without wobbling.
    - Keep the throttle at a steady RPM and avoid over-revving, as sudden acceleration can cause instability.

- Practice riding in congested areas to familiarise yourself with this exercise in real-world scenarios.

U-turn:

One of the parts of this test that requires good control is the U-turn section. The U-turn part of the motorcycle test, which you will need especially in normal road conditions, such as parking lots or when reversing when you are going the wrong way on the road, aims to test your ability to manoeuvre in a limited area. Here you will be asked to make a full U-turn without putting your feet on the ground and without crossing a specified width limit (usually 7.5 meters).

- **What to Expect:** The examiner will ask you to make a controlled U-turn without putting your feet on the ground within the area that shown to you, usually an area demarcated by two lines on the sides.

- **Key Tips:**

  - After you start riding and before you begin the manoeuvre, determine the direction you will be traveling by looking over your shoulder toward the direction of the turn.

  - Use the clutch and gas together to regulate your control and avoid sudden movements and maintain a **steady speed**.

  - Keep your gaze towards where you want the motorcycle to go, looking away towards the direction of the turn will help you steer the motorcycle smoothly.

  - Practice U-turns frequently in car parks or open areas to build confidence in riding the motorcycle at slow speeds.

Controlled stop:

Controlled stopping, which is one of the most common situations encountered in daily riding scenarios, is an important skill that you will use especially in situations such as when the vehicle in front of you slows down and stops in normal traffic, when giving way at pedestrian crossing, or stopping when you come to traffic lights.

For a controlled stop, you will be asked to stop smoothly and definitely at a designated point after accelerating to approximately 20 mph.

- **What to Expect:** You will ride forward and reach a specified speed of approximately 20 mph, then stop smoothly and controlled in a designated line.
- **Key Tips:**
  - Stop smoothly without jerking, using both **front and rear brakes** equally.
  - Reduce the throttle as you slow down and apply light pressure to the brakes.
  - On motorcycles with gears, don't forget to engage the clutch when slowing down to prevent your motorcycle engine from completely stalling when you slow down too much and are about to stop.
  - Practice stopping smoothly at various speeds, especially in parking lots or in areas closed to traffic that you find suitable, to improve control.

Emergency stop:

When you encounter an emergency situation where you may need to stop quickly to prevent a sudden accident while riding a motorcycle, what you need to do is to apply your "emergency stopping" skill. The important issue tested in this section in emergency stops is your reaction time when you encounter such situations on the motorcycle and your ability to stop quickly without losing control of the motorcycle.

During this part of the test, the examiner will signal you to stop suddenly from approximately **31 mph (50 km/h)**. If you are taking the test on a moped, this speed requirement is reduced and you will need to reach a speed of at least **19 mph (30 km/h)** before making emergency stop.

- **What to Expect:** When the examiner gives you the signal, usually by raising hand or as shared with you before you start, you will be required to stop the motorcycle immediately. Proper timing and brake control are especially critical in this section.
- **Key Tips:**
    - Apply **firm pressure** on both the front and rear brakes at the same time.
    - Keep your arms relaxed but hold the handlebars firmly to avoid losing control when stopping.
    - Stop without locking the front wheel by gradually increasing the brake pressure to ensure a smooth deceleration.
    - To improve sudden stops, practice stopping in an emergency at approximately the desired speed,

especially in parking lots or areas closed to traffic that you find appropriate.

Hazard avoidance:

The hazard avoidance test is one of the vital parts when faced in real life and combines some of the features of the previous controlled stop and emergency stop, and also assesses your ability to manoeuvre around a hazard at a given speed.

In this exercise, you will accelerate to 31 mph (19 mph for mopeds) and manoeuvre to avoid a hazard, usually represented by a cone or cones, and then come to a controlled stop.

- **What to Expect:** The examiner will ask you to go towards a cone at a speed of at least 31 mph and then come to a stop under control before stopping the motorcycle.
- **Key Tips:**
    - Using the counter-steering technique will help you here, pushing the handlebars in the opposite direction of the turn to quickly move the motorcycle away from the hazard, thus manoeuvring away from the danger.
    - When your speed increases, hold the throttle steady until you pass the hazard and brake gently to stop smoothly without skidding or stalling.
    - Work on hazard avoidance in closed traffic areas to gain confidence in controlling the motorcycle during sudden changes of direction.

- Always look beyond the hazard instead of focusing directly on it, remember that the motorcycle tends to go where you look, this will help you steer the motorcycle smoothly around the hazard.

4.2.2 MOD 1 MARKING AND PASS CRITERIA

The marking system in Mod 1 is determined by the number and type of faults you make during the test. There is a certain tolerance for minor errors called "riding faults" in the test, but more than 5 minor faults may cause you to fail the test.

More critical faults are considered serious or dangerous, the test is not generally terminated in the event of critical fault, but at the end of the test, the examiner will inform you that this fault is serious or dangerous and that you will not pass as a result of this type of fault, even if you did everything else correctly. Therefore, you should try to minimise minor errors and avoid **serious** or **dangerous faults** altogether.

- **Minor (Riding) Faults:** These are minor mistakes, such as a slight hesitation during a manoeuvre or a little lack of control. A few of these mistakes will not prevent you from passing the test, but making a large number of minor riding faults (more than 5) will show that you have a lack of control of the motorcycle or understanding of the rules, which may cause you to fail the test.

- **Serious Faults:** These are errors that endanger both your safety and control of the motorcycle, such as not performing a manoeuvre correctly or not following the instructions properly. If you make even one of these faults, your test will fail.

- **Dangerous Faults:** Any action that endangers you or others, such as losing control of the motorcycle, performing critical manoeuvres such as emergency stops or avoiding danger in a dangerous and incorrect manner, will automatically result in you failing the test. In this case, depending on the extent of the danger, the examiner may decide to stop the test immediately.

Minimum Speed Requirements:

In Mod 1, you must follow specific speed limits that are required during the emergency stop and hazard avoidance sections. Upon reaching a specific speed, it is essential to show that you are capable of these manoeuvres:

- **Emergency Stop:** You must reach a speed of at least 31mph (19mph for mopeds) before the stop signal is given by the examiner.

- **Hazard Avoidance:** Similarly, you will need to reach a speed of 31mph (19mph for mopeds) and be able to quickly and move away from a hazard in control before making a safe stop.

Failure to reach the required speeds during these exercises will be considered a fault and repeated failure to meet these speed requirements will result in you failing the test.

Key Point:

The Mod 1 test is carried out in a safe closed to traffic area at a DVSA test centre, **not on public roads**. The test will simulate some real riding conditions and you will be expected to demonstrate that you have full control of your motorcycle throughout the test.

Code: 46000d

The circuit layout diagram for the Mod 1 test is the same across all test centres and can be downloaded from the official gov.uk website **Motorcycle Manoeuvring Left and Right Circuit Diagrams** PDF by scanning the QR code on the side. Downloading this document will help you to familiarise yourself with the circuit in advance, allowing you to better understand the test environment and prepare for the test day.

4.3 MODULE 2 (MOD 2): ON-ROAD RIDING TEST

Location: On public roads near the DVSA Test Centre.

The aim of Mod 2 is to prove that you can ride safely and in a controlled manner in various traffic situations. There was a controlled area in Mod 1, but the colour of the situation changes in Mod 2. The test, in which you will do real riding on public roads, in traffic, will last approximately **40 minutes** and you will perform this riding on various roads, from residential areas to busy roads, from roundabouts to dual carriageways.

4.3.1 WHAT HAPPENS IN MOD 2

Eyesight check

Eyesight Check before the test starts, you will be asked to read a number plate from a distance of **20 metres** (**20.5 metres** for old-style plates). You are legally required to have sufficient vision from this distance. If you cannot read the plate, the test ends there and you fail. Always check your eyes before the test and do not forget to bring your glasses or contact lenses if necessary.

Safety Questions: The "Show Me, Tell Me"

After the eyesight check, the examiner will ask you two safety questions. The first is known as "**Tell Me**" and the other is known as "**Show Me**".

- **Tell Me:** This question will ask you to answer questions that relate to basic motorcycle safety and maintenance, such as how you check brakes, tyre pressure, or oil levels. In short, you are expected to demonstrate your ability to check that your motorcycle is roadworthy and safe.

- **Show Me:** In this question, the examiner will ask you how to operate the brake lights, signals or other important controls on the motorcycle, so that you know whether you are familiar with the motorcycle you are testing on and can use it if you need it when you set off. On the other hand, sometimes the really important parts of the motorcycle you are testing on are also tested to see if they work safely.

To help you prepare for these questions, you can find an official list of "Show Me, Tell Me" questions that you may encounter on the test by scanning the QR code on the side. Be sure to review these questions before going to the test, this will help you feel comfortable during the test.

Code: 59c317

On-road riding

At this point, your road ride will begin and you will set off under the supervision of an examiner who will follow you on a motorcycle or another vehicle. Instructions will be given to you via a one-way radio headset (in the unlikely event that this will be a two-way radio communication device). At this stage, the examiner will evaluate how you adapt to traffic, how you move in different road scenarios, and the structure of the test will include tasks such as two normal stops, an angled start, and if possible, a hill start.

4.3.2 KEY ELEMENTS OF THE ON-ROAD TEST

When you come to the road test of Mod 2, the serious part can begin. Here, the examiner will evaluate your ability to use the motorcycle in real traffic conditions and your compliance with the road rules.

Some basic elements to be evaluated in the test will be listed below:

General Road Riding:

During the test, the examiner will observe how you use the motorcycle in different road conditions and will do this on a route such as **residential streets**, **urban areas** and **dual carriageways**. You must show that you ride the motorcycle smoothly and confidently, both with your motorcycle control and body movements, by paying attention to all road signs, speed limits and traffic lights.

- **Speed Control:** You must maintain your speed in accordance with the speed limits of the road and traffic conditions, you should definitely not go above the speed limit and not too low under.

- **Observation:** You should show that you are aware of other road users by frequently checking your mirrors and especially your blind spots (shoulder checks) before turns.

- **Positioning:** Position yourself correctly by staying in the correct lane as much as traffic and signs allow, and avoid unnecessary lane changes.

- **Signalling:** Use signals correctly when making turns or changing lanes, do not forget to turn off the signal after the manoeuvre is completed.

Independent Riding

At some point during the test, the examiner will ask you to ride **independently**, following road signs in the direction they have given you. The aim is to assess your ability to navigate the road safely on your own without constant guidance. It will take around **10 minutes** of your Mod 2 test.

- **Key Focus:** Here, rather than your ability to follow the exact route, your ability to interpret road signs correctly, anticipate hazards and safely control the motorcycle will be evaluated. Even if you take a wrong turn on the road, the evaluation will not be whether your turn is wrong, but whether you can do it safely.

- **Tips:**

    - **Clarify Before You Start:** Before you set off, ask the examiner if there is any uncertainty about any directions or instructions. Once you have started riding, it is always best to clarify in advance to avoid confusion, as communication between you is usually one-way radio communication.

    - **Lost During the Ride:** If you make a wrong turn depending on the traffic conditions while riding independently, don't panic. The examiner expects you to ride safely, he/she is not looking for perfect navigation skills, you will not fail just because you got lost.

- **Dealing with Lost Situations:** The examiner will usually explain to you in advance before you start the test what to do if you get lost or separated from them. In most cases, if you lose them, you will be told to **pull over and wait** for the examiner to catch up. However, if this has not been discussed from the beginning, ask the examiner what to do if this happens and make it clear.

Junctions and Roundabouts

Navigating **junctions** and **roundabouts** correctly is an important part of riding on the road in the UK and an important part of this test. The examiner will carefully monitor your checking mirrors, signals and lane positioning as you approach and pass these areas.

- **Approach:** Reduce speed when approaching junctions and roundabouts, checking your mirrors and blind spots as you do so. Give the appropriate signal after the mirror check to make your intentions clear.

- **Positioning:** Pay particular attention to the directions written on the road or on signs to stay in the correct lane, especially at multi-lane roundabouts and junctions. These will help you determine which lane you should be positioned in before entering the junction.

- **Observation:** Constantly observe situations such as oncoming traffic, cyclists, pedestrians preparing to enter the road at the side of the road. Try to constantly pay the same attention to observation here as you did in the hazard awareness section of the theory test.

Overtaking and Lane Changes

The examiner will observe how well you manage overtaking and lane changing in real traffic conditions and whether you do so safely and efficiently.

- **Observation:** Check your mirrors and blind spot before changing lanes or overtaking, and perform a proper shoulder check (a lifesaver) just before them.

- **Timing:** Before overtaking or changing lanes, make sure that the road and the action you want to take are safe, then avoid being in too much of a hurry or acting with too much hesitation.

- **Signalling:** Always remember to signal before changing lanes or turning at a roundabout, but do not forget to cancel the signal after making your turn.

Hazard Awareness

One of the things the examiner pays most attention to in the Mod 2 test is how well you can **anticipate and respond** to potential hazards on the road, such as parked cars, pedestrians, cyclists and other vehicles.

- **Anticipation:** Look ahead to spot potential hazards early. For example, if you see a parked car ahead, plan ahead to safely pass it.

- **Adjustments:** Adjust your speed and position as necessary. For example, if there are pedestrians on the roadside or in a narrow street, it is appropriate to slow down and continue riding in a safe position.

- **Decision-Making:** The examiner will observe whether you make safe choices, for example, whether you wait for a safe gap in traffic or whether you refrain from overtaking when it is inappropriate.

Other Aspects

- **Road Signs and Traffic Signals:** The examiner will observe whether you obey all road signs and traffic signals such as stop signs, give-way signs, speed limits and traffic lights, and if you do not notice these signs or do not follow the rules, this will be considered an error in the eyes of the examiner. Always think in your head, "**This is my test track, every sign is important here**" and do not forget to pay attention to all signs.

- **Following the Highway Code:** As part of the test, the examiner will expect you to demonstrate a safe and considerate riding style in accordance with the Highway Code, for example, showing respect for others on the road, paying attention at pedestrian crossings and complying with road signs and traffic signals.

- **Dealing with Traffic:** Whether you are riding on quieter roads or in crowded city traffic, you will be expected to ride calmly and confidently during the test. This will involve being able to travel safely in stop-and-go traffic, and reacting to fast-moving traffic on dual carriageways. It is also OK to filtering, but as the test does not measure this skill, reconsider filtering which may increase risk of fault, even within legal restrictions.

- **An Important Tip:** Put yourself in the examiner's shoes throughout the test. They will want to see a rider who is aware of their surroundings, safe, and complies with the rules. If you act in accordance with this expectation, this test will not seem as difficult as it seems.

4.3.3 MOD 2 MARKING AND PASS CRITERIA

In the **Mod 2** test, the scoring system is similar to **Mod 1**; you can pass the test even if you make some **minor faults** (riding faults), but if you make **serious** or **dangerous faults**, as in Mod 1, you will immediate fail. The examiner will monitor your riding along the way, observing your level of control, awareness and safety, and will assess you on this basis.

Minor Faults (Riding Faults)

The **minor faults** you make during the **Mod 2** test ride will not mean that you will fail the test on their own. This will be interpreted as small errors that show that there are areas of improvement in your riding. There is only one exception here; if you repeat the same small mistake frequently, then it may be considered a lack of skill and result in a negative result in your test.

Examples of minor faults could include:

- **Slightly early, late use of signals:** Giving signals too early or a little late before making a turn may not directly create a big danger, but it can indicate a lack of timing and attention to what is happening on the road.

- **Hesitating unnecessarily at junctions:** Even if it does not affect the traffic flow at junctions or roundabouts, stopping unnecessarily and doing this frequently while entering the junction can indicate that you are making poor decision in terms of traffic and positioning.

- **Slight deviations in lane positioning:** Not being able to stay in an ideal position in the lane can also be evaluated negatively in terms of your stance on the road. This is even more important, especially in critical areas such as junctions and roundabouts, as such positional deviations can also create a danger in terms of traffic.

- **Inconsistent mirror or shoulder checks:** Not checking your mirrors regularly or forgetting to do a shoulder check when changing lanes will be considered a mistake, but when this happens repeatedly, it can be interpreted as you are not paying enough attention to what is happening on the road and do not normally care about this issue, and it can have negative results.

Although you can pass the test with **up to 10 minor faults** overall, the frequency of some faults may make a minor fault to serious fault even if your overall count of minor faults are less than 10.

Repeated minor faults: For example, frequently forgetting to cancel indicators or hesitating at every junction can be seen as a lack of skill and confidence in the decisions you make while riding, which will lead to a failed test result.

Critical areas: Faults made in critical areas such as decision-making at junctions, your observation skills, and speed control can negatively affect the test outcome. When the examiner identifies these faults, they may interpret them as a sign that your awareness of your surroundings is not complete, which could be assessed as a serious fault and result in a failed test.

Minor faults are not defined by strict and absolute rules, but their assessment largely depends on the examiner's interpretation of how the faults you make affect your riding safety. The examiner will always expect a safe, controlled, and confident ride rather than perfection.

As I mentioned in the minor faults section, if you repeatedly make the same minor fault, the examiner may interpret this as a serious issue with your overall riding skill or awareness. In such cases, even if they are not serious, minor faults may collectively lead to a failure, so try to avoid repeating the same mistakes as much as you notice them during your ride.

Serious Faults

A serious faults can be defined as one that should not be made to pass the test and which endangers your safety or that of other road users. If you make a single serious mistake of this kind, it will be considered a significant weakness in your riding technique or judgement and will result in a failure.

Some examples of serious faults include:

- Failing to make observations at junctions or roundabouts that could lead to a collision.
- Not giving way when required by road signs or markings.
- Misjudging the speed or position of other vehicles when overtaking or changing lanes, endangering those in traffic.
- Experiencing speed control issues such as riding over the speed limit, riding too fast when conditions require a slower speed, or failing to adjust speed when approaching hazards.

- Demonstrating lane discipline problems, such as drifting between lanes or not staying in the correct lane at roundabouts.

Serious faults will indicate potential risks in your riding and will be interpreted by the examiner as a need for additional training or experience.

Dangerous Faults

Making a mistake that endangers yourself or others while riding is called a dangerous fault in Mod 2 tests for the safety of road users, and it is of great importance for examiners to be careful in preventing possible accidents that may arise from such mistakes.

Examples of faults to watch out for are such as:

- Disobeying a traffic light or a stop sign.
- Merging into traffic from a junction, without observation of the surroundings.
- Engaging in dangerous overtaking.
- During the test of the motorcycle if you lose control by skidding or not being able to stop in a situation.

Showing a dangerous fault indicates an inability to maintain control or awareness which could suggest to the examiner that you may not be fully prepared for the challenges of riding in public areas.

Before your Mod 2 test begins and to ensure you are well prepared and aware of what to expect during the assessment process and how to enhance your performance in every aspect reviewed; simply scan the QR code for access to the official guide

Code: bd248e

understanding your motorcycle Mod 2 test results, in case of errors or faults encountered during the test attempt or if a retest is required.

4.4 WHAT HAPPENS AFTER THE TESTS?

- **Mod 1 Results:** You will receive the results of your Mod 1 test immediately after you have completed it, if you have passed you can book your Mod 2 test. If you fail you will need to re-book Mod 1 and re-take the test after working on the areas you found difficult. If you are upgrading your licence via '**progressive access**' you will need to **pass Mod 2 within 6 months**. If you fail to complete within this period of time, you will need to re-book and re-pass Mod 1.

- **Mod 2 Results:** Similarly you will be notified of the results of your Mod 2 test as soon as you have completed it. Passing both Mod 1 and Mod 2 means you are now eligible for a full motorcycle licence and your new licence will be sent to you by the DVLA (Driver and Vehicle Licensing Agency).

4.5 RETAKING THE TEST

If you fail any section of the Mod tests, which are practical tests, you can retake the test after **3 working days**.

If you have already scheduled your Mod 2 test and failed Mod 1, you may need to reschedule your Mod 2 test date. This is because you need to pass Mod 1 before moving on to Mod 2. Please bear in mind the cancellation and amendment policy; failure to give at least three full working days' notice will result in your test fee being forfeited. So if you want to book both Mod 1 and Mod 2 at the same time, please allow at least 3-5 days in between to allow for changes in case of any problems.

Although the minimum requirement for retaking the exam is 3 days, use this time to correct any mistakes you may have made in the feedback provided by the DVSA and continue to work until you feel more confident before retaking the test. If you are short on time and not feeling confident, it may be worth postponing your test date a little further.

4.6 TIPS FOR SUCCESS

Passing both Mod 1 and Mod 2 requires good preparation, confidence and the right mindset.

Here are some important tips for acing your test:

Practice, Practice, Practice

Your mastery of the manoeuvres on your motorcycle, especially in **Mod 1**, will improve with frequent repetition. You will also need to practice controlling your motorcycle at low speeds, especially in tight turns, balancing when riding between tight turns and slalom cones or doing figure eight manoeuvres. The more you practice, the more comfortable you will feel during the exam and the more successful you will be.

- **Key Focus:** Work on developing your throttle and clutch control to ensure smooth and stable movement at low speeds. Work on developing your muscle memory for stopping correctly at certain points, perfecting your U-turns and avoiding emergency stops and hazard avoidance.

Get Professional Training

While personal practice is certainly one of the most important aspects, professional training will give you an extra edge in your practice as the instructor will alert you to any mistakes you may have made or were unaware of during your personal practice. Many riding schools offer courses specifically designed to prepare you for both **Mod 1** and **Mod 2**. These courses will allow you to practice on tracks that are similar to those at DVSA test centres, simulating test conditions, and will help you to correct any shortcomings you may have, with constant feedback from the course instructors.

- **Benefits:** Professional instructors will provide constructive feedback, helping you to identify areas for improvement that you may not have noticed on your own. They will also give you access to test standard motorcycles, similar tracks and conditions, so you can get used to the real test conditions.
- **What to Look For:** Try to choose a training centre with experienced instructors and good reviews from previous students. Many training centres offer short "intensive" courses that focus solely on preparing you for the Mod 1 and Mod 2 tests. Google reviews are particularly effective in the UK, and checking these will help you choose the right course for you.

Stay Calm and Focused

As with any test, it is natural to feel nervous on the day of the test, but what you need to do to succeed is to try to stay calm. When you are not calm, your tense nerves can lead to mistakes, so take a deep breath, focus on the road and remember that the examiner does not expect perfection, but controlled and safe riding.

- **Mindset Tips:** Break the exam into small, manageable sections in your mind and focus on the task at hand, not on what is coming next. If you make a small mistake, do not dwell on why you made it; unless it is a serious or dangerous mistake, it may not result in failure, just trust yourself and try not to make the same mistake again. As I mentioned before, mistakes are small and there is no problem; only repeated mistakes can negatively affect your test result.

- **Relaxation Techniques:** Do deep breathing exercises before the exam, visualise a smooth, successful ride. Try to use the experience you have gained from preparing for the things you need to do slowly but confidently and by practicing.

Ride Defensively

Defensive riding will ensure that you are always aware of what is happening around you and that you position yourself to minimise risk whilst maximising your visibility to others. Defensive riding is critical to **Mod 2** and safe riding in general motorcycle riding life. The examiner will watch and assess how well you anticipate and position yourself for the actions of other road users, potential hazards and unexpected situations.

- **Key Defensive Skills:**

  - **Observation:** Regular mirror checks, shoulder checks (life-savers) and constantly scanning the road ahead are the most basic and vital observation points.

  - **Anticipation:** During your Mod 2 ride, constantly try to anticipate the events in front of you and to your side, namely the behaviour of drivers, cyclists and pedestrians. For example, if you see a car at a junction, anticipate that it may come out and adjust your speed or position accordingly.

  - **Positioning:** Stay in a safe lane position that gives you room to manoeuvre if something unexpected happens. For example, being in a position where you can be seen in the mirror of the vehicle you are riding behind will make drivers ahead aware of your presence in their own manoeuvres.

- **Extra Tip:** Don't just focus on completing the test route; showing the examiner that you are aware of your surroundings and proactive in anticipating hazards will help convince them that you are a safe rider in these conditions.

In this chapter, I explained about the final stages of becoming a licenced motorcyclist, the Mod 1 and Mod 2 tests, and what kind of work you need to do. After completing this final stage, you will begin your adventure on two wheels in the UK in the category of your licence. Be sure that you will successfully complete this task when you listen to the tips and advices here.

5. PREPARING YOUR MOTORCYCLE AND YOURSELF FOR THE ROAD

Whether you're preparing for your practical tests or just getting ready for your daily ride, it's essential to make sure your motorcycle is fully road-ready for both legal and practical purposes before you start riding. In this chapter, I will try to share some relevant information on the essential elements needed to ensure your motorcycle is roadworthy, safe and compliant with UK regulations.

5.1 MOTORCYCLE EQUIPMENT CHECKLIST: ENSURING ROADWORTHINESS

A well-maintained motorcycle is important for passing your tests, and also for riding safely and complying with UK law. Regular checks on your motorcycle, even if they are taking short time to check, will help prevent mechanical failure and reduce the risk of accidents. Going out on a ride with the confidence that your motorcycle is in tip-top shape will also increase your confidence in your own riding and your motorcycle.

Below I have tried to compile a list of the essential components that you should check regularly to keep your motorcycle safe and roadworthy.

5.1.1 TYRES

Your tyres are one of the most critical components of your motorcycle. Proper tyre care ensures better handling, improved grip, and overall safer riding.

- **Tread Depth:** The legal minimum tread depth for motorcycles over 50cc is **1mm** across three-quarters of the tyre's width. For mopeds under 50cc, the original tread grooves must remain visible around the entire tyre.

- **Condition:** Inspect the tyres for cracks, punctures, or signs of uneven wear. These could indicate alignment or suspension issues that need attention.

- **Pressure:** Ensure your tyres are inflated to the manufacturer's recommended pressure. Under-inflated tyres can reduce your handling and increase wear, while over-inflated tyres can make your ride harsh and affect traction.

5.1.2 LIGHTS

The lights on your motorcycle are very important for visibility, both for you to see the road in low light conditions and for others to see you. Correct and complete operation of lights is an important aspect of road safety and is a requirement under UK law.

- **Headlights and Tail Lights:** Before setting off, especially in low light conditions, test both your **high** and **low beam**s to make sure they are working properly.

- **Indicators:** Check that all indicators are flashing properly and can be seen from a distance.

From time to time, the visibility of your lights may be reduced due to mud after rainy weather, in this case, even if you do not wash your motorcycle completely, be sure to clean all dirty lights before setting off.

5.1.3 BRAKES

The brake system is vital to your motorcycle, as it is to any moving vehicle. For safe riding, check your brakes, and always test your brakes before starting each ride.

- **Brake Pads:** If you see that the brake pads are worn and that they are very thin, plan to change them immediately to prevent deterioration of brake performance and danger.

- **Brake Fluid:** Be familiar with the brake fluid locations on your motorcycle, and make sure that the brake fluid is filled to the required level and free of contaminants. If the fluid is low or dirty, it can reduce the effectiveness of your brakes, so plan to change or add brake fluid.

- **Testing Brakes:** Always test both the **front** and **rear brakes** before each ride to make sure they respond quickly and effectively.

5.1.4 MIRRORS

Your mirrors are important equipment that you will use to increase awareness of other road users, especially those on the sides and behind you, to control the environment for the actions you will take, and to be prepared for unexpected situations. Good mirror adjustment helps reduce blind spots and allows you to make safe lane changes.

- **Secure Fit:** It is important for your mirrors to be clean and fixed as you have adjusted them for safety. Make sure your mirror is fixed, motionless, and free from dirt and cracks that may obstruct your vision.

- **Proper Adjustment:** When you get to your motorcycle, the mirrors may change direction due to impact and someones touching compared to cars, adjust them to have a clear and comprehensive view behind you before you get on. As a tip, it is especially important to check the mirror alignment before your practice test to demonstrate good road awareness.

5.1.5 HORN

A working horn is essential to alert other road users to your presence in potentially dangerous situations. In this case, noticing that your horn is not working could have dire consequences.

- **Operational Check:** Always test your horn before each ride to make sure it is working. Your horn should be loud enough to be heard by pedestrians and other vehicles in your immediate vicinity, and if you notice a decrease in volume, you should plan to have it repaired as soon as possible.

5.1.6 CHAIN AND SPROCKET

If your motorcycle has a chain and sprockets (some have belt or shafts instead of chains), you should properly maintain this equipment, which is responsible for transferring power from your engine to the wheels, otherwise it may cause poor performance or even accidents such as chain breakage.

- **Chain Slack:** You can check if there is excessive slack or tightness in the chain by hand or with simple tools (they called "chain tension tools") developed for this purpose. While a loose chain can usually slip and throw off the sprocket, an overly tight chain can damage the drivetrain or even result in the chain breaking.

- **Lubrication:** Regularly lubricating your chain to reduce friction and prevent premature wear will allow you to use your chain more efficiently and for a longer period of time.

- **Sprocket Condition:** The chain will naturally wear out on the sprockets while the motorcycle is in motion, no matter how frequent it is lubricated. Check regularly if these signs of wear or damage are above the specified limits. Worn sprockets will lead to poor power transmission and possible mechanical failures.

Taking good care of your motorcycle by performing these checks regularly will not only protect you, but will also keep others on the road safe. Make these inspections a habit and always refer to your motorcycle's manual for maintenance instructions specific to the model of motorcycle you are using.

5.2 LEGAL REQUIREMENTS: TAX, MOT, INSURANCE, AND VEHICLE REGISTRATION

To use your motorcycle legally in the UK, the legal requirements are to pay tax on the vehicle, have a valid MOT and have the correct insurance cover.

5.2.1 MOTORCYCLE TAX

- **Road Tax (Vehicle Excise Duty)** is mandatory for all motorcycles used on public roads.
- The **tax responsibility** varies depending on how you purchased your motorcycle:
    - **If it was purchased outright:** You are responsible for paying the vehicle tax.
    - **If you are on a PCP (Personal Contract Purchase):** Although the vehicle technically belongs to the credit company until the last balloon payment is paid, you are liable for taxes on the motorcycle since you are registered keeper of it.
    - **If you are on a lease:** In this case, the leasing company will usually be shown as the registered keeper and unless otherwise stated in the lease agreement, the leasing company pays the tax.
- Always check your contract to see if you are liable for road tax as you could face fines and legal action if you do not pay your tax.

5.2.2 MOT

- If your motorcycle is over 3 years old, it is mandatory to have an annual MOT test.
- The MOT assessment will check key components such as lights, brakes, steering, suspension and emissions.

- With these components in mind, it is important that your motorcycle is in good condition and complies with MOT standards, not only for legal reasons but also for your safety.

5.2.3 INSURANCE

- **Insurance** with at least third party cover is mandatory for all motorcycles to be legally ridden on UK roads.

- The type of insurance policy you need to choose will vary slightly depending on how you buy your motorcycle:

    - **Outright ownership:** You have full control over the type of insurance and provider, and can choose any type of insurance you want here.

    - **PCP or Finance Agreement:** Usually the finance company will expect your insurance to cover the full value of the motorcycle to protect their investment in the event of an accident or theft. Check your finance agreement for any requirements regarding cover.

    - **Lease:** You will usually need to arrange full comprehensive insurance as specified in the contract with the leasing company.

5.2.4 VEHICLE REGISTRATION

- Your motorcycle must be properly registered with the DVLA (Driver and Vehicle Licensing Agency).

- If you are the registered keeper (even under a finance agreement), it is your responsibility to ensure the vehicle is registered in your name unless it is a lease.

5.3 MOTORCYCLE MAINTENANCE BASICS

Regular maintenance is essential to ensure a safe ride, performance, and to avoid costly repairs in the future. In this section, I will try to provide some simple and some more meticulous DIY (Do-It-Yourself) tips and alternatives that will help with routine maintenance.

5.3.1 OIL CHECKS

Oil is critical to engine health because it lubricates, cools, and cleans your motorcycle's engine. Ensuring that the oil is at the right level and quality will ensure that your motorcycle's engine is efficient and has a long life.

- **Checking the Oil Level:** Check the oil level regularly using your motorcycle's oil dipstick or sight glass. When performing this check, it will help you get a more accurate measurement if the motorcycle is level, that is, not leaning to one side with the side stand.

- **Top-Up and Oil Changes:** When the oil level is low, you can add the type of oil recommended by your motorcycle manufacturer. In general, a full oil change will be healthier, but you can add oil in order not to leave your engine without oil due to lack of time. It is important to use the type and quality of oil recommended in your motorcycle model booklet, otherwise choosing the wrong oil may cause problems with engine performance and increased engine wear.

- **Regular Oil Changes**: Follow the motorcycle manufacturer's recommendations for oil change intervals. For most motorcycles, oil should be changed approximately every 3,000-5,000 miles, or more frequently if used in extreme conditions, but as I mentioned, your motorcycle manufacturer may specify a different time, so be careful about the frequency.

5.3.2 BRAKE FLUID LEVELS

Brake fluid is also important for protecting the brakes and ensuring their proper response. Therefore, it is very important to check them regularly and replace them if they are lacking or damaged, for your safety while riding.

- **Monitor Fluid Levels:** Check the levels in both the front and rear brake fluid reservoirs regularly for signs of low fluid levels. Low brake fluid could be a sign of brake pad wear or a possible leak.

- **Fluid Replacement:** Brake fluid absorbs moisture from the air and the environment over time, which can affect the brake performance of your motorcycle. Change brake fluid at the intervals recommended by the motorcycle manufacturer, usually every 1-2 years. Use the type of fluid specified by the motorcycle manufacturer's owner's manual, usually every 1-2 years. The type of brake fluid is usually brake fluid with a DOT rating of 3, 4 or 5.1.

- **Bleeding the Brakes:** Air bubbles can sometimes accumulate in brake fluid, which can reduce braking efficiency. For this reason, it may be necessary to bleed the brakes. You can bleed your brakes yourself as a DIY job, but if you are not confident in doing it yourself, you can have a professional do it.

5.3.3 TYRE PRESSURE

If you want good handling and long tyre life, you should definitely check that your tyres are at the correct pressure, especially before long rides.

- **Use a Reliable Gauge:** You can use a tyre pressure gauge to make sure your tyres are within the pressure range recommended by the motorcycle manufacturer. Remember that any changes in pressure values can affect your handling and braking performance.

- **Check When Cold:** Tyre pressure should be checked when the tyres are cold, that is before you start riding or after you have waited for your tyres to cool down for a while, as the heat from riding can increase the pressure readings.

- **Consider a Portable Inflator:** Having a small portable tyre inflator will be very useful for long rides or tours. Portable inflators, especially those with batteries, are both space-saving and very practical on long trips. A portable inflator will be very helpful on rural rides or especially if you find a service station nearby, as their inflators sometimes do not work.

5.3.4 CHAIN MAINTENANCE

A motorcycle uses different systems such as chain, belt and shaft for power transmission. However, most motorcycles use chains for power transmission. If your motorcycle is has chain, proper chain maintenance is vital. A poorly maintained chain can cause problems such as poor performance, wear on other components and therefore increase the risk of mechanical failure.

- **Clean and Lubricate Regularly:** Debris and dirt accumulate on the chain over time and regular cleaning is very useful to prevent chain wear that may occur due to these. After cleaning, lubricate your chain so that it reaches the inside of the chain links.

- **Adjust Chain Tension:** Correct chain tension is important for smooth gear shifting. A chain that is too tight or too loose can cause handling problems and even mechanical problems, and can also reduce the life of the chain and gears.

- **Auto Lubing Options:** To facilitate chain maintenance, you can consider lubrication systems such as **Scottoiler** or **Tutoro**, which technically extend chain life and reduce maintenance frequency by providing **automatic chain lubrication** while riding.

5.3.5 ADDITIONAL TIPS AND ALTERNATIVES

Battery Maintenance

The battery is a vital component that powers the lights, gauges, and other electronic devices that are used to start the motorcycle in the first place.

- **Regular Checks:** Loose connections on the battery can cause the motorcycle to lose power due to the vibrations while riding, which can compromise riding safety. Check the battery connections for corrosion and make sure they are tight. You can clean any corrosion with a mixture of baking soda and water, then apply a light coat of grease to protect against corrosion.

- **Battery Charger:** You can use a trickle charger or smart battery charger to keep your battery charged, especially if you don't ride regularly all year round. This is a practical solution to avoid completely draining the battery, which can cause permanent damage over time.

- **Consider Lithium-Ion Batteries:** If you're looking for a low-maintenance option, consider lithium-ion batteries, which have become popular in recent years. These batteries hold their charge longer and are lighter than traditional lead-acid batteries. However, lithium batteries may not fit every motorcycle, so check with the manufacturer before doing this to make sure it is compatible with your motorcycle.

Spark Plug Inspection

Spark plugs play an important role in the engine's ignition using fuel and overall performance.

- **Check for Wear:** Inspect the spark plugs for signs of wear, such as black or white deposits on them or damaged electrodes; if any appear worn or damaged, that means it is time to replace them.

- **Use the Correct Gap:** For optimum performance, make sure the spark plug gap matches the motorcycle manufacturer's recommendations.

Coolant Checks

When your motorcycle is running, it will start to warm up while riding. If your motorcycle is liquid cooled (air cooled motorcycles are also available), coolant is used to help regulate engine temperature and prevent overheating.

- **Top-Up When Needed:** If the coolant level in the reservoir is low, be sure to top up with the type of coolant recommended by your motorcycle manufacturer.

- **Change Coolant Periodically:** Old coolant can become ineffective and will not be able to properly regulate engine temperature. So change it every 1-2 years to keep your engine at operating temperatures.

Regular maintenance activities can help you ensure that your motorcycle runs as it should, thereby improving your road safety and lowering the likelihood of unexpected breakdowns.

5.4 RIDING GEAR: CHOOSING THE RIGHT SAFETY GEAR

Wearing the right riding equipment is critical for both safety and comfort, and some are even legally required to be worn. In the event of an accident, proper equipment can significantly reduce the severity of injuries.

Additionally, high-quality equipment can provide weather protection, keeping you comfortable and relaxed in a variety of conditions, and helping to ensure that your riding experience is not compromised by clothing. In this section, I will share the equipment options that are essential to maximise your safety and riding experience.

5.4.1 HELMETS

The most important piece of protective gear for motorcyclists is the helmet, as it provides critical head protection. Choosing the right helmet can sometimes make the difference between minor injuries and serious head trauma in the event of an accident, so it pays to take great care when choosing your helmet.

- **Legal Requirement:** In the UK, as of the date of writing, it is mandatory to wear a helmet that meets British Safety Standards (BSI) BS 6658:1985 or equivalent European standards. The helmet you purchase must have a minimum **ECE 22.05** label confirming that it has passed rigorous safety tests.

- **Types of Helmets**:

    - **Full-Face Helmets:** These are helmets that offer the highest level of protection, covering the entire head, face and chin. In crash situations, full face helmets are considered the most reliable and protective option, they are recommended for all weather conditions and high speed riding. They are especially preferred for high-risk sports riding.

    - **Modular Helmets:** Also known as flip-up helmets, modular helmets offer a balance between protection and comfort. Recently developed modular helmets offer high safety, but due to their modularity, they carry small risks compared to full-face helmets. The most important advantage of these helmets is that they can cover your entire head and at the same time, they can help you communicate more easily or breathe more comfortably by moving a part of it whenever you want. It is usually a model preferred by those who want to stop and communicate frequently on long tours or in the city.

- **Open-Face Helmets:** While open face helmets provide less protection than full-face helmets and modular helmets, they offer better ventilation and are popular for slower, city rides. However, since they leave the face open, they are less safe because they do not have a part that will prevent you from getting hit in the jaw and face in the event of an accident.

- There are also helmets that do not provide much safety other than meeting the legal requirement, such as some half-shell helmets, but here I wanted to talk about helmets that are more standard in terms of safety.

- **Additional Tips**:

  - **Fit and Comfort:** Your helmet should fit your head and face without causing discomfort, especially in the forehead and cheek areas. A well-fitting helmet that fits tightly without slipping is very important for safety. Proper fit is important in terms of reducing fatigue, and less fatigue will also make your ride safer and better quality. Try different helmet sizes and shapes that suit your head size and shape, not every popular helmet will fit your head, this fit may vary by brand.

  - **Visor Options:** Choosing the right visor can improve both your safety and comfort. Focus on visors that are scratch-resistant and can be fitted with anti-fog or anti-fog inserts (**Pinlock**) to ensure clear vision in a variety of conditions. Here are some of the visor types that come with helmets or that you can purchase separately:

- **Tinted or Photochromic Visors:** Tinted visors reduce glare and are useful for daytime riding, especially in sunny weather, but only visors with **at least 50% light transmittance are legal in the UK**, meaning extremely dark visors are illegal in low-light conditions. You can only use these for off-road activities on track days. Photochromic visors that automatically adapt to light changes, that is darken when the sun is out and lighten when the sun is out, can be a versatile alternative, but you need to make sure that these visors meet the legal requirements.

- **Clear Visor for General Use and Night Riding:** In general, it is best to carry a clear visor or wear it in the evening, because visibility is very important for safety and darker visors are not suitable for night riding by law. If the sun bothers you on public roads, you may want to consider a helmet with sunglasses or a sunglass feature.

• **SHARP Rating**: In the UK, the **SHARP (Safety Helmet Assessment and Rating Programme)** system is an organisation that constantly tests helmets and provides a safety rating. Helmets

Code: eec593

are rated from one to five stars based on impact tests at various speeds and angles. When choosing a helmet, it will be important for your safety to choose helmets with a high SHARP rating (preferably four or five stars) as they provide better impact protection rather than visual looking. The SHARP rating system offers additional insights beyond the basic certifications, and you can check their website for these details by scanning the QR code on the side.

In general terms, choosing your helmet by prioritising fit, choosing a visor that is appropriate for the conditions and ensuring that your helmet provides maximum safety and comfort in line with UK regulations by considering the SHARP ratings will help you ride more safely.

5.4.2 JACKETS, GLOVES, BOOTS, AND TROUSERS

Each of these components plays a role in protecting different parts of the body in the event of a fall or accident, helping to minimise injuries.

- **Jackets:**

  A quality motorcycle jacket will not only protect you in the event of an accident, it will also shield you from the weather.

  - **Armour Protection:** Choosing a jacket with **CE-approved armour** on key impact points such as the back, shoulders, and elbows is important for safety. Some jackets come with some protection as standard, while others are optional. So pay attention to what protection comes with the jacket, and if possible, try to get a jacket with removable armour. Removable armour allows you to upgrade the protection or remove it for washing.

- **Materials:** Leather is a natural, and sometimes synthetic, material that offers excellent abrasion resistance. Its high abrasion resistance makes leather a preferred choice, especially for high-speed riding. For better versatility, textile jackets made of materials such as **Kevlar** or **Cordura** also provide good protection, are usually waterproof and can be worn in layers in colder weather. Therefore, such jackets are also a practical choice for long distances and daily use.

- **Weather Adaptability:** Especially if you ride a motorcycle in summer and winter, a jacket with a removable thermal lining and a waterproof layer will be in place for cold or rainy conditions. Some quality textile jackets have ventilation options compared to leather, which is a good option to prevent overheating in warmer weather.

- **Gloves:**

Gloves protect your hands from impacts and improve grip, even in the slightest fall, if you do not have gloves on, your hands are the most prone to injury. In this respect, using gloves in summer and winter will be important for your safety.

- **Fit and Protection:** Gloves should be tight but not so tight that they restrict your access to the controls. While choosing gloves with reinforced joints, padded palms and wrist protection, try to choose gloves that do not restrict access to the controls.

- **Seasonal Considerations:** For winter riding, try to choose gloves that provide thermal insulation and waterproofness. Summer gloves will provide adequate protection while also providing ventilation and will help you not to experience problems in hot conditions. In this respect, you may sometimes see gloves under the name of 3 or 4 season gloves. Unfortunately, a single glove cannot usually meet all seasonal conditions, so depending on your usage, it would be a logical decision to buy one summer and one winter or 3-season gloves together.

- **Boots:**

Motorcycle boots protect your feet and ankles while balancing on a variety of surfaces, whether wet, slippery, asphalt or dirt.

- **Ankle and Shin Protection:** Boots should at least cover your ankles, as they are one of the first to reach the ground in the event of a fall or potentially if the motorcycle tips over onto your feet. With many options available, you can also find boots with shin guards for added impact protection.

- **Grip and Sole:** Try to get boots with non-slip soles to maintain traction on wet or slippery surfaces. Boots usually have reinforced toes and heels to help protect your feet in the event of an accident.

- **Waterproofing:** Waterproof boots are of course a must for the unpredictable weather in the UK, as you can ride through rain and puddles without waterproof boots, which can make your ride uncomfortable.

- **Trousers (Pants):**

While protective trousers may not come to mind as much as jackets, they will protect your lower body, especially your knees and hips, which are vulnerable in the event of an accident.

- **Armour Protection:** Choose trousers with **CE-approved armour** on your knees and hips, as these areas are at the highest risk in the event of a fall. Many trousers offer pockets for adding or upgrading armour, as do jackets.

- **Materials:** Leather trousers, or even full-coverage overalls, are preferred for faster rides, offering high levels of abrasion resistance. For a more versatile and comfortable use, consider **reinforced riding jeans** made of materials such as Kevlar, which offer a good balance between protection and comfort. While they resemble natural everyday jeans, they also provide good protection thanks to armour in certain areas. Textile options, which usually include water-resistant and breathable fabrics, are also a good choice, especially for long distances and daily, all-season urban use.

- **Weather Adaptability:** Some trousers come with thermal linings for warmth, which you can remove in warm weather. Waterproof or water-resistant trousers are also a good option for all-weather riding, while in the warmer months, trousers with ventilation panels to prevent overheating are a sensible option.

5.4.3 ADDITIONAL PROTECTIVE GEAR

In addition to helmets, jackets, gloves, boots and trousers, other protective equipment can increase your safety and comfort.

- **Reflective Gear:**
    - Reflective jackets, vests or armbands will significantly reduce the risk of accidents by increasing your visibility to other road users during night riding or in low visibility conditions such as rain or fog. You can wear these types of vests over your existing jacket when necessary, as they do not take up much space.
    - Many jackets and trousers now come with integrated reflective panels, although not as much as reflective jackets and vests. You can also choose such a jacket as a design in mind.
- **Back Protectors:** While some jackets come with built-in back armour, some jackets have a back pocket section, but you may need to buy it separately rather than with the jacket. For higher impact resistance, if you are going to buy a new back armour, prefer **CE Level 2 protection**.

- **Weather Accessories:** For colder months, battery-powered neck warmers, heated gloves or heated jacket liners can help you ride comfortably. In the summer, a cooling vest or moisture-wicking base layers may be preferred to stay cool during long rides.

5.4.4 FINAL TIPS FOR MAXIMISING SAFETY AND COMFORT

When selecting the appropriate gear, it is important to make an effort to find a balance between protection, comfort, and adaptation to the varied weather conditions that can be experienced in the UK.

I would like to share some final advice that you should keep in mind:

- **Invest in Quality Gear:** High-quality equipment may not always, but is generally, more expensive; however, it will usually last longer and provide better protection. Make sure to read online user reviews before making a decision on these items.

- **Layering:** Layering your clothing will help you adapt to different weather conditions, helping you stay comfortable in all conditions. Wearing a thermal base layer in the winter and lightweight, moisture-wicking materials in the summer will help you continue riding comfortably.

- **Inspect Regularly:** Check your gear regularly for wear and tear, especially in high-impact areas like your helmet, gloves, and boots. Try not to drop your helmet, especially since the materials in your helmet are made of shock absorbers that are sensitive to impacts. Try to replace worn or damaged gear, for example, a damaged waterproof boot may no longer be waterproof.

By choosing the right equipment and maintaining it as necessary, you will not only ensure compliance with UK safety standards but also ensure protection and comfort regardless of the riding conditions.

5.5 MODIFYING YOUR MOTORCYCLE: LEGAL LIMITS AND INSURANCE IMPACT

Modifications that you may want to make to your motorcycle, whether for visual or performance reasons or to draw attention to aesthetics, are among the issues that should be implemented with caution, as they may affect both the legal compliance of your motorcycle and your insurance policy.

Before you make changes, you must first understand the legal and insurance implications to avoid these problems or creating unsafe riding conditions.

In this section, I'll share the main areas of modification that could impact both.

5.5.1 LEGAL LIMITS ON MODIFICATIONS

In the UK, modifications to your motorcycle may render it illegal for public road use if they don't meet the required safety and compliance standards. Here I will share some common changes and their legal considerations:

- **Exhaust Systems:**
    - **Noise Limits:** The upper exhaust noise limit for new motorcycles over 175cc in the UK is **80**

(dB) decibels (75 dB up to 80cc, 77 dB for 81 - 175cc). Replacing your exhaust with one that increases noise above these decibel levels can lead to fines and failing your MOT test.

- **Emissions Standards:** The changes you make must be within the emission standards set for motorcycles in the UK. For example, if you have a new motorcycle purchased after 2021, the exhaust you want to change will need to comply with the Euro 5 emission standard. Depending on the year and consumption of your motorcycle, the emission application in the UK varies, so it would be useful to check the emission standards suitable for your motorcycle. For example, replacing or removing the catalytic converter in a way that increases your motorcycle's emissions figures above legal limits could render your motorcycle unroadworthy.

- **Lighting:**
    - **Headlights and Tail Lights:** When making any changes to your motorcycle's headlights or taillights, you must use products with the **E-marked**, which shows that they comply with EU regulations. Inappropriate lighting could lead to fines and problems with your MOT test.
    - **Coloured LED Lights:** With coloured LEDs proving popular, it may seem tempting to add them as underbody lighting, but they can be illegal on UK roads. Using them on a motorcycle can lead to fines and penalty points, as red, blue or flashing lights are strictly reserved for emergency vehicles.

- **Daytime Running Lights (DRLs):** Any aftermarket DRLs you fit must comply with the legal regulations to ensure they do not blind other road users. You need to make sure they are E-marked and aligned correctly so they do not irritate oncoming traffic.

- **Mirrors:**
    - In the UK, if a motorcycle has mirrors originally fitted by the manufacturer, you must keep mirrors on the motorcycle. Removing existing mirrors and fitting aftermarket mirrors that do not meet visibility standards can result in a fine, failing an MOT test or causing problems in an accident.

- **Indicators:**
    - UK law requires all motorcycles used on public roads to have functional indicators if originally fitted by the manufacturer. If these are subsequently replaced, the indicators must be E-marked and fitted at a visible height and angle. Small or coloured aftermarket indicators may not meet legal visibility requirements and you may still encounter UK legal and MOT issues.

- **Number Plate Size and Position:**
    - Plates are designed to specific size and font requirements in the UK. Aftermarket plates with smaller or different fonts are illegal and may result in fines or vehicle seizures. The

letters and numbers on the plate must be positioned well so that they are clearly visible from behind without obstruction.

5.5.2 INSURANCE CONSIDERATIONS

Modifying your motorcycle may affect your insurance policy as it can change the risk profile of the motorcycle.

Modifications you make will usually increase your insurance premiums, if you do not report these changes the insurance company may not cover your claim if you need insurance as a result of a problem.

- **Reporting Modifications:**
    - **Mandatory Disclosure:** You must notify your insurance company of any modifications you make to your motorcycle, regardless of size. If you failure to report modifications could result in your claims being denied in the event of an accident, theft or any other incident, which could put you in a difficult financial situation.
    - **Policy Cancellation:** In some cases, if the modifications you make significantly increase the insurance risk level, the insurance company may cancel your policy.
- **Premium Adjustments:**
    - **Increased Premiums:** If the modifications you make increase your motorcycle's speed, power or make it more visually appealing, the insurance company will generally increase your premiums because they think there will be a higher probability of theft or accidents.

  - **Reduced Premiums:** Adding security-enhancing features such as **immobilisers** and **tracking systems** can often reduce the risk of theft, potentially lowering your premium. For this, you can consult your insurer and choose security equipment approved by your insurance company.

  - **Changes in Coverage:** Some insurers may limit coverage for modified motorcycles, with restrictions on certain areas (such as track use), so check your policy terms to make sure your modifications are covered.

- **Documentation and Proof:**

  - **Keep Receipts and Photos:** If you make changes, be sure to keep receipts and before and after photos of the changes you made. This documentation will help prove and convince you if there are questions about the value or legality of your changes in the event of an insurance claim.

  - **Professional Installation:** Many insurers may want to have professionals install high-value modifications or safety-critical modifications so they can verify their value. Before making any changes, it would be a good idea to talk to your insurance company to clarify whether you need professional installation.

- **Effect on Market Value:**

  - Some modifications can increase the resale value of your motorcycle and some can decrease it. Insurers will often not cover the full increased value resulting from changes unless it is stated in your policy. In this respect, it would be useful to keep in mind that you may not be able to receive financial compensation from insurance for the changes you make.

In this chapter I have shared information on the essential elements required to ensure your motorcycle is roadworthy, safe and compliant with UK regulations. Once you have considered what is written here you can continue riding with peace of mind.

6. INSURANCE, TAX, AND MOT FOR MOTORCYCLES

There are legal and financial things you need to think about once you own a motorcycle and start riding it. In this part, I share about the basics of UK insurance, road tax, and MOTs. I will also share about how much it costs to own a motorcycle over time.

Whether you own your motorcycle outright or have a payment plan like a PCP, it's important to know what your legal and financial obligations are so you can stay in line and keep costs low.

6.1 UNDERSTANDING MOTORCYCLE INSURANCE

Motorcycle insurance is a legal obligation designed to protect you, your motorcycle and others in the event of an accident, theft or damage, with different coverage types in the UK as in many countries. When determining insurance coverage, it would be a good insurance selection strategy to try to achieve the coverage you are looking for and at a cost that will meet your expectations.

In this section, I will try to gather with you the main types of coverage, the factors affecting premiums, and tips for choosing the best policy.

6.1.1 TYPES OF MOTORCYCLE INSURANCE

Third-Party Insurance

- **Coverage:** The minimum insurance you are required to take out under UK law is Third Party Insurance. This is the type of insurance that covers damage to the person, vehicle and property of third parties in the event of an accident and you are at fault as a result of the accident.

- **Limitations:** This type of insurance will not cover damage to your own motorcycle or injuries to you, as only the third party is covered in accidents caused by your fault, meaning you will have to pay for any repairs to your motorcycle or personal medical expenses out of pocket.

- **When to Consider:** This type of insurance may be preferred for people with low-value motorcycles or especially for new motorcycle licence holders in order to consider high insurance premiums. However, you will need to keep in mind that while it provides a budgetary advantage, it provides limited protection that does not cover your damages in return.

Third-Party, Fire, and Theft (TPFT)

- **Coverage:** TPFT is a slightly expanded type of insurance that, in addition to third-party protection, also covers theft or fire damage to your motorcycle.

- **Limitations:** As with third-party insurance, this type of insurance will not cover damage to your motorcycle or personal injury in an accident where you are at fault.

- **When to Consider:** TPFT would be a good option, especially if you have a mid-level motorcycle and want to protect your investment, including the risks of theft or fire through no fault of your own.

Comprehensive Insurance

- **Coverage:** The type of insurance with the highest level of cover is comprehensive insurance. This is an important type of insurance that covers you for third party, fire and theft, as well as your own motorcycle and any injuries you may sustain in an accident, whether the fault lies with you or someone else.

- **Additional Protections:** Many comprehensive policies can also cover vandalism, natural disasters and other unforeseen events. Since there may be differences between insurance companies that offer comprehensive policies, it will be useful to check these in your policy.

- **When to Consider:** Comprehensive insurance is particularly ideal for new, high-value motorcycles or when your motorcycle is financed through PCP or lease agreements. This is because financial agreements in particular often require comprehensive cover to protect the lender's investment.

6.1.2 FACTORS AFFECTING PREMIUMS

Although insurance premiums vary depending on various factors, I will try to share some elements that you can control or change to reduce costs.

- **Age and Riding Experience:** Younger and inexperienced riders often face higher premiums as they are statistically more likely to be involved in accidents. If you are young and inexperienced, you cannot immediately increase your age and years of experience, so an advanced riding course (such as **IAM RoadSmart** or **RoSPA**) can reduce your premiums by demonstrating your commitment to safe riding.

- **Motorcycle Model:** From time to time, new and inexperienced riders attempt to buy high-performance, sports or luxury motorcycles without considering the insurance premiums, and then when they try to get insurance, they face higher premiums due to the increased risk. Especially if you are a new rider, you can catch low costs both as a motorcycle and insurance premiums by turning to cheaper, lower-power models and reduce your insurance costs.

- **Location:** In urban areas, unfortunately, high premiums are paid due to increased theft and accident rates. If you live in a high-risk area, it would not be a very logical and economical move to change where you live when you buy a motorcycle, but storing your motorcycle in a secure garage or using a tracking device will help reduce the high premiums a little more.

- **Annual Mileage:** The more you ride, statistically, the greater the risk of an accident. Especially if you correctly determine not the miles you will not do during the year, but the miles you will actually estimate, you can also save money here.

- **Security Features:** Adding security features such as alarms, immobilisers, chains or disc locks can reduce your costs in some insurance companies. Many insurers can reduce your insurance premiums by offering discounts, for example, when you use Thatcham-approved safety equipment.

- **No-Claims Discount (NCD):** No claims discount, although not used in the first year of ownership of your motorcycle, will reduce your premiums in subsequent years for each year that you do not claim. Some insurers offer additional policy features for NCD protection that can allow you to retain your discount even after making a small claim, it is worth looking into these and including them in your insurance where necessary.

6.1.3 CHOOSING THE RIGHT INSURANCE

To choose the most suitable insurance policy for you, you will need to understand how you use your motorcycle, its value and your specific needs. Here I will try to share some tips to tailor a policy that suits you:

- **For Financing Options:** If your motorcycle is financed through a **PCP (Personal Contract Purchase)** or lease agreement, comprehensive insurance will usually be required by the lender. They will usually specify this to you in the finance agreement. This is intended to enable finance companies to protect their own assets and cover repairs in the event of an accident.

- **Optional Add-Ons:**

    - **Personal Injury Cover:** This is a cover available in some policies that covers medical expenses related to injuries sustained in an accident, regardless of fault. This is especially useful if you are looking for additional protection in the event of an accident with high coverage in case of injuries.

- **Legal Expenses:** No one wants to be involved in an accident, but sometimes accidents will occur as a result of unexpected events. In this case, one of the items that is usually neglected is the issue of legal expenses. It is an additional insurance item that covers the costs of legal representation if you are involved in a dispute after an accident. You cannot know in advance whether you will have a dispute in case of an accident, but it will be useful to add this additional coverage as a precaution.

- **Helmet and Leathers Cover:** This additional coverage protects your riding equipment. This coverage, which usually has a small additional cost to the insurance, can be advantageous for riders with high quality or specialised equipment.

- **Breakdown Cover:** Although standard breakdown cover is included in some motorcycle insurances, it is usually not very comprehensive and helpful. Therefore, especially if you are going to ride long distances or commute daily, you can definitely use services such as RAC and AA, which are specialised in this field, which have additional or even external breakdown cover. These will get you out of a difficult situation when you have a breakdown thanks to their support such as roadside repairs, towing or rescue.

6.2 MOTORCYCLE ROAD TAX

Motorcycles, like cars, are subject to taxation on UK roads. The cost of this tax varies according to the size of your motorcycle's engine size. It is a legal obligation to pay your motorcycle tax, so you may be penalised if you do not.

6.2.1 HOW TO CALCULATE AND PAY YOUR ROAD TAX

Your motorcycle is taxed according to the engine size and this is arranged to be paid every year.

- **Engine Size Categories:**
    - **Up to 150cc:** Motorcycles with a smaller engine size benefit from a lower tax rate, low tax rates and easy access to CBT make motorcycles of this size particularly desirable to own in the UK. Especially the low tax rates will be an ideal option for new riders and commuters.
    - **151cc and Above:** Tax rates for large motorcycles of 151 cc and above are divided into three parts: 151-400 cc, 401-600 cc and 600 cc and above. Due to the emissions of the engine volume of each motorcycle and the greater road impact, a different tax rate has been determined, which increases as the engine volume increases.
    - **Electric Motorcycles:** If you currently own a fully electric motorcycle, you will be exempt from road tax until **1 April 2025**, which will give you the advantage of cost savings. However, from 1 April 2025, electric motorcycles will be taxed at an annual rate for

the smallest engine size and from that date all motorcycles will be taxed, regardless of whether they are electric or not.

- **How to Pay:**

    - **Payment Frequency:** You can pay the road tax **annually**, **semi-annually** or **monthly** at automatic payment frequencies with Direct Debit, or you can pay manually annually without automatic payment.

    - **Payment Methods:** You can pay online via the **DVLA's website** (you can access via scanning the QR code on the side) or in person at a Post Office. Online payment is generally very convenient and you can follow up very easily without physically visiting a place.

Code: 20d397

6.2.2 TAX RESPONSIBILITY BASED ON OWNERSHIP

Your tax liability on your motorcycle will vary depending on the type of ownership or the financing arrangement on the motorcycle. Depending on these types, sometimes you may be responsible and sometimes the finance companies may be responsible.

- **Owned Motorcycle:** If you own the motorcycle outright, you are solely responsible for paying the tax as the registered owner.

- **PCP (Personal Contract Purchase):** If you own a motorcycle with the PCP model, you will be liable for tax as the registered keeper, even though the finance company technically owns the motorcycle. There may be exceptions to this model, so it would be useful to read your contract in this respect.

- **Lease Agreement:** If you are using the motorcycle with a lease, the finance company will pay the tax as the leasing company will usually be the registered keeper. However, it will still be useful to check your contract to see who is responsible for the tax. Although it is unlikely, you may also be responsible for tax in some cases in this model.

6.2.3 CONSEQUENCES OF NOT PAYING

If you do not pay the road tax, you can face serious penalties.

- **Fines:** Failure to pay road tax can result in a fine of up to **£1,000**.

- **Clamping and Impounding:** Your motorcycle can be clamped or seized if it is spotted on public roads without the current tax paid.

- **Scrapping:** In extreme cases, if seized as a result of unpaid tax and you fail or ignore instructions as notified to you by letter, your motorcycle will be treated as abandoned and may lead to it being scrapped by the authorities.

6.3 MOT REQUIREMENTS FOR MOTORCYCLES

In the UK, motorcycles over three years old are subject to an annual MOT (Ministry of Transport) test to ensure they meet safety and environmental standards. Before you take your motorcycle for an MOT test, completing any deficiencies and understanding what is checked during the test will help your motorcycle to pass the test successfully by ensuring that your motorcycle remains roadworthy.

6.3.1 WHAT IS CHECKED DURING AN MOT?

During the MOT, a certified technician will inspect the various components of your motorcycle. In particular, I will try to briefly explain the general issues prioritised by the MOT test here.

- **Lights and Indicators:** All lights must be in full working order, including headlights, tail lights, brake lights and signalling lights. On the other hand, as it is important that your lights are correctly aligned so as not to dazzle other road users, alignment checks will also be carried out.
    - **Tip:** Before the test, check that all lights on your motorcycle are in working order and replace any defective bulbs. It will also be useful to check the light alignment settings of your motorcycle without a load before you go.
- **Brakes:** To ensure that your motorcycle's brakes are in good condition and provide effective stopping power, the MOT test will check all components of your front and rear brake systems such as brake pads, discs and brake fluid levels.
    - **Tip:** Check your brake fluid levels regularly, topping them up if they are low and replacing brake pads if they are worn. These are also components that you should constantly check for your safety.

- **Steering and Suspension:** Check your brake fluid levels regularly, topping them up if they are low and replacing brake pads if they are worn. These are also components that you should constantly check for your safety.
    - **Tip:** Inspect your suspension for leaks or cracks, especially after long rides or if you have travelled over rough terrain. If you can make this a regular habit, it will help you fix problems before they become more serious.
- **Tyres:** Motorcycles over 50cc are required by MOT test and by law to have at least **1mm** across three quarters of the tyre width. For mopeds under 50cc, the original tread grooves must be visible all around the tyre. On the other hand, regardless of the engine size of your motorcycle, there should be no cracks or bulges on the tyre.
    - **Tip:** Regularly checking your tyres for cracks, tread depth and bulges and making sure they are inflated to the recommended pressure will be beneficial for both your safety and the MOT test.
- **Exhaust:** Make sure that your exhaust system does not make excessive noise and is within the legal emissions for the engine size, especially if you have replaced the exhaust produced by the manufacturer within the legal limits for your engine.
    - **Tip:** Avoid modifications to your exhaust that may increase noise levels beyond the legal limit, as these will directly lead to MOT failure, so it will be beneficial to choose an exhaust system that will consistently meet these requirements.

- **Horn and Mirrors:** The horn should be loud enough to warn other road users and mirrors should be of a shape and size that allows you to see the road clearly behind you.

    - **Tip:** Always test that the horn is working properly and adjust the mirrors to provide the best visibility before you go for your MOT test, as you don't honk all the time in normal use.

6.3.2 PREPARING FOR THE MOT

Regularly maintaining your motorcycle will reduce the risk of unexpected failing an MOT test.

- **Regular Maintenance:** Regularly check your brake pads and replace them if they are worn. Replace tyres with new ones if they have low tyre tread. Correct common problems such as faulty lights, which can be solved simply, with regular checks. Keeping a maintenance programme to follow regularly will help you to identify and resolve any potential faults that may arise during the MOT in advance.

- **DIY Checks:** Before the test, carry out a DIY inspection of critical components such as your motorcycle's lights, horn, tyres and mirrors to try to identify any problems beforehand. After identifying them, you can make the fixes yourself, if there are corrections you cannot fix by yourself, you can get support from a professional.

- **If Your Motorcycle Fails:** If your motorcycle fails the MOT test, you will need to fix the problems before the re-test. Some MOT centres offer a free re-test to fix the problems within a certain period of time and go back to the same test centre again, so it will be useful to ask the MOT test centre about this issue.

6.4 THE COST OF MOTORCYCLE OWNERSHIP

At first, the cost of owning a motorcycle may be perceived as just the purchase price of the motorcycle. In fact, understanding the ongoing costs beyond the purchase price of the motorcycle will help you budget more effectively and avoid unexpected costs.

6.4.1 INSURANCE

Annual insurance premiums vary widely, ranging from **£200 to over £1,000**, depending very much on factors such as the type of motorcycle, where you live, the level of cover, how long ago you have held your motorcycle licence and your age. As I have already explained in previous sections, comprehensive policies will be more expensive, but they do offer wider protection.

Tip: You can find a suitable policy by using websites that compare multiple quotes each year. For each year that you do not have any claims from the insurance, you will have no-claims discounts, you can get more advantageous prices by adding them to your policy enquiries.

6.4.2 ROAD TAX

Most motorcycles will fall into the tax bracket of £25 to £117 per year depending on engine size as of the date I write. You can find the current road tax figures using the QR code on the side.

Code: be3626

Tip: Electric motorcycles are exempt from road tax at the time of writing, but this exemption will expire on **1 April 2025**. From this date the lowest motorcycle engine size will be levied as a tax, which will continue to keep them as a cost-effective option for a limited time.

6.4.3 MOT

From the time your motorcycle is three years old it will cost an annual MOT, which will be approximately **£30 to £50**. You can find the current maximum cost of MOTs by scanning the QR code on the side.

Code: 594f6d

Tip: During the winter months, when appointment availability is usually higher, MOT centres can sometimes offer discounts, which you can take advantage of to save money.

6.4.4 SERVICING AND REPAIRS

Regular servicing is one of the most important aspects of keeping your motorcycle running properly for many years. Depending on the age of the motorcycle and the complexity of the work to be carried out, your approximate cost will be between **£100 and £500** per year, sometimes more.

Tip: For older motorcycles, it may be necessary to have them serviced more frequently as some components may start to cause problems and cost now that the warranty has expired. You can allocate a budget for possible repairs, especially considering the potential additional cost of owning an old motorcycle.

6.4.5 FUEL COSTS

Fuel costs depend on the frequency of riding, the efficiency of the motorcycle and sometimes also on whether maintenance is carried out properly:

- **Smaller Bikes:** Typically get **70-100 mpg**, making them an economical choice for commuters.
- **Larger Bikes:** Usually achieve a consumption value of around **30-50 mpg**, which will increase costs on long journeys.

  Tip: Regular maintenance such as inflating tyres to the correct pressure, oil and chain maintenance will improve fuel efficiency and reduce costs.

6.5 BREAKDOWN COVER: A MUST-HAVE FOR PEACE OF MIND

Breakdown cover is not legally compulsory. However, it is a wise additional cover, especially for riders who travel long distances or use their motorcycles to commute to work.

6.5.1 WHAT DOES BREAKDOWN COVER INCLUDE?

Breakdown cover usually includes the following basic services:

Roadside Assistance: If your motorcycle breaks down, a mechanic will come to your location and try to fix it on the spot.

> **Tip**: Many providers offer phone apps that allow you to quickly request help and give you information about when a mechanic will arrive.

Recovery: If on-site repair is not possible, the mechanic will arrange for your motorcycle to be towed to a nearby garage or home. This is one of the most important forms of assistance, especially when stranded.

> **Tip:** Some policies offer a towing service to a location of your choice if you are away from home, you can plan this by checking the details of your policy.

Home Start: If your motorcycle won't start at home, a mechanic can come to help and provide assistance at home.

> **Tip:** This is a very useful and much-needed service, especially in winter, as the cold weather can affect your motorcycle's battery. This service may not be included in every policy, so it would be useful to look for additional coverages.

Onward Travel: If your motorcycle cannot be repaired immediately, policies are also available that offer alternative transport options such as rental vehicle or public transport.

> **Tip:** If you use your motorcycle for commuting or travelling, you should strongly consider adding this feature.

6.5.2 COST OF BREAKDOWN COVER

- Breakdown cover varies depending on the level of service you choose, usually costing between **£50 and £150** per year.
- Many insurers, or the company you buy your motorcycle from if you have just bought a new one, offer breakdown cover as an additional cover, sometimes at a discounted rate, which will simplify your cover management.

6.5.3 BENEFITS OF BREAKDOWN COVER

Failure cover offers several particularly important advantages:

- **Financial Protection:** Without coverage, towing will generally be expensive and the fees will often exceed the cost of the annual policy, which is one of the key advantages that lead to obtaining this coverage.
    - **Tip:** Breakdown cover is a more cost-effective insurance option for roadside repairs and towing than outsourcing the service individually.
- **Convenience and Safety:** Breakdown cover means you won't be stranded if something goes wrong and you'll get help quickly, which is especially important for night or rural riding where it can be more difficult to get help.
    - **Tip:** If you're a frequent motorcyclist, it's worth choosing a comprehensive policy that includes home start and ongoing travel for maximum peace of mind.

In this chapter, I have tried to give additional information and tips about the legal and financial responsibilities of motorcycle ownership in the UK by choosing the right insurance, going over the tax and MOT requirements in detail. When you apply these, you will be able to go on more comfortable rides.

7. THE UK MOTORCYCLE HIGHWAY CODE: WHAT YOU NEED TO KNOW

Understanding the rules set out in the UK Highway Code is as important for motorcyclists as it is for all road users. In this section I will endeavour to provide useful information specifically for motorcyclists, covering the basic rules, responsibilities and best practice so that you can ride safely on the road.

Code: 9c3564

Important Tip: I have tried to design this chapter as a useful practical guide, I strongly recommend that you read the official document by scanning the QR code for the full and official Highway Code.

7.1 ESSENTIAL ROAD RULES FOR MOTORCYCLISTS

If you are riding a motorcycle in the UK, you should follow the general rules of the road, but you should also observe specific guidelines tailored specifically to two-wheeled vehicles. In particular, being aware of the rules of speed limits, overtaking, filtering and roundabout navigation will help you stay safer and avoid possible fines or penalties.

7.1.1 SPEED LIMITS

Motorcyclists in the UK are required to obey the same speed limits as cars, except in designated areas where special motorcycle-specific limits may apply. You should always be aware of your speed and pay attention to signs indicating speed limit changes and adjust the speed of your motorcycle accordingly.

Standard Speed Limits:

- **30 mph** in built-up areas (usually the presence of street lights indicates this standard speed when no speed sign is posted). If there are different speed practices in such built-up areas, this will be indicated on the speed sign.

- **60 mph** on single carriageways roads (with no central reservation/centre lane to separate each direction).

- **70 mph** on dual carriageways and motorways.

Key Tips:

- **Adjust Speed in Adverse Conditions:** As weather conditions in the UK are constantly changing, especially if you are riding four seasons, in wet, icy or foggy conditions; it is better to choose a slower pace to maintain traction and reaction time.

- **School Zones and Residential Areas:** In areas where speed limits are lower, especially during school hours, or in areas with heavy pedestrian traffic, try to pay extra attention to the signs by paying attention to your speed.

- **Rural Roads:** These roads are generally quieter and national speed limits may apply, but they can often be narrow. There may be hidden hazards such as sharp bends, farm vehicles or debris in the road, so try to choose a safer, slower speed rather than travelling at the national speed limit.

7.1.2 FILTERING (LANE-SPLITTING)

Filtering (also called lane splitting) is a method of moving your motorcycle between lanes of slow moving or stationary traffic. It is legal in the UK if you do it safely, but it is important for your safety and the safety of other road users to be careful as car drivers may not expect motorcycles to pass them in this way.

Rules and Tips for Safe Filtering:

- **Filter at Slow Speeds:** The Highway Code recommends filtering at low speeds, generally not exceeding 15-20 mph above the speed of traffic, to give greater control and reaction time.

- **Watch for Sudden Lane Changes:** Since car drivers may change lanes especially in heavy traffic unexpectedly, you can adjust your position and speed by paying attention to their signal lights and wheel movements.

- **Avoid Filtering Near Junctions:** Avoid filtering close to junctions, roundabouts or driveways where vehicles are more likely to turn or change direction.

- **Keep Safe Distance**: As big vehicles like buses and trucks have considerably greater blind zones, make sure you have enough space between you and the cars on either side of you and try to avoid getting too close.

7.1.3 OVERTAKING

For motorcycle riders, overtaking may not look much different from normal car overtaking, but due to the motorcycle's agile mobility, it is important that timing and awareness control are needs to be very accurate.

Overtaking Rules and Tips:

- **Overtake on the Right:** In the UK, as in most island countries, overtaking is on the right, unlike in mainland countries (not all but most of them). An important point that some car and motorcycle drivers/riders overlook is that undertaking (passing on the left) is prohibited unless traffic is moving slowly and vehicles in the right lane are moving slower than your lane.

- **Avoid Overtaking Near Junctions or Crossings:** Since the likelihood of other vehicles crossing your path can be high at junctions, blind spots and pedestrian crossings, not overtaking in such places will reduce the risks.

- **Check Your Mirrors and Blind Spots:** Check your mirrors before overtaking and always do a shoulder-check before passing to make sure there are no vehicles in blind spots. Since this is a vital action for motorcyclists, making it a habit will help you in terms of your safety.

- **Avoid Overtaking on Bends or Hill Crests:** Especially on single-lane or single-track roads, it will be useful to avoid overtaking in these areas, as oncoming vehicles or dangers can be hidden on bends, hill crests.

- **Leave Enough Space:** When passing other vehicles, leave enough space between you and them to avoid hitting mirrors or handlebars and to avoid potential hazards. In particular, this will help you to avoid the danger of wind turbulence that can destabilise your motorcycle when overtaking large vehicles, or to be prepared for sudden unaware manoeuvres by drivers.

7.1.4 ROUNDABOUT RULES

Roundabouts are a common feature of UK traffic and an important component of the UK's traffic system, helping to speed up the flow of traffic by reducing the number of traffic lights. It is worth mentioning some techniques to ensure that you can pass safely and smoothly on your motorcycle, just as you would in a car.

Approaching the Roundabout:

- **Position Correctly:** Stay in the lane in the direction you want to turn, if you are going straight, check the direction signs (sometimes on the road surface) to see which is the correct lane. Some larger roundabouts may have lane guidance signs before the junction, in which case you can use these signs to decide which lane to stay in.

- **Anticipate the Exit:** Identify your exit as early as possible as you approach the roundabout and try to adjust your position gradually as you come to the junction so that you do not have to change lanes at the last minute and can make your turn more safely.

Using Signals:

- **Make Your Intentions Clear:** Signal your intentions before exiting the roundabout, this will allow drivers/ riders following behind to understand your intentions and adjust their position and speed if necessary, resulting in a safer exit.

- **Maintain Signal Awareness:** Especially at multi-lane intersections, pay attention to signals from other vehicles to avoid problems due to unexpected sudden lane changes by other vehicles.

Additional Roundabout Tips:

- **Watch for Pedestrians and Cyclists:** Many roundabouts have crosswalks at the entrance and/or exit. Be prepared even from a distance to slow down or stop for pedestrians or cyclists, as they may cross.

- **Keep Your Speed Low:** Although roundabouts help flow, not stop, like traffic lights, they are designed for low speeds, not high speeds. Therefore, approach with caution to maintain control, especially in wet or slippery conditions.

- **Be Aware of Larger Vehicles:** Although larger vehicles such as trucks or buses may be in their own lane before making a turn, they need extra space to pass, especially at tight roundabouts. Keep a considerable distance, especially if you are around them, and try not to overtake them at roundabouts.

7.2 USING BUS LANES

You can use some bus lanes in the UK with your motorcycle, but the rules vary from borough to borough, especially in London. In London, when you cross between boroughs while the bus lanes continue uninterruptedly, you may unfortunately find that some boroughs do not allow motorcycles in the bus lanes.

So always pay attention to the road signs and make sure there is a **motorcycle figure** in the **bus lane signs**. Here are some examples at the time of writing:

In **Westminster**, you are allowed to use your motorcycle in most bus lanes, but when you move to **Camden**, the rules change and some bus lanes are not allowed for your motorcycle.

In **Southwark**, bus lanes allow you to use your motorcycle in the bus lanes, but in **Lambeth** the restrictions are different.

Because of these inconsistencies, even when riding your motorcycle in continuous bus lanes that span multiple boroughs, you will need to pay attention to signage or you could face unexpected fines.

Note: There are campaigns by different motorcycle action groups to standardise bus lane rules across the boroughs, but at the time of writing the rules remain inconsistent.

7.3 TRAFFIC SIGNS AND SIGNALS

As a motorcyclist, you should be familiar with all traffic signs, but some of the most common ones are particularly important.

There are many signs to be aware of, but here are a few important ones to summarise:

- **Roundabout Signs:**
    - Among the signs you may see when riding to junction, especially **large roundabouts**, you may see the sign that guides you which lane to use for the different exits. Since such roundabouts usually have more than one lane, it will help you to decide which lane to stay in by deciding your exit point in advance.

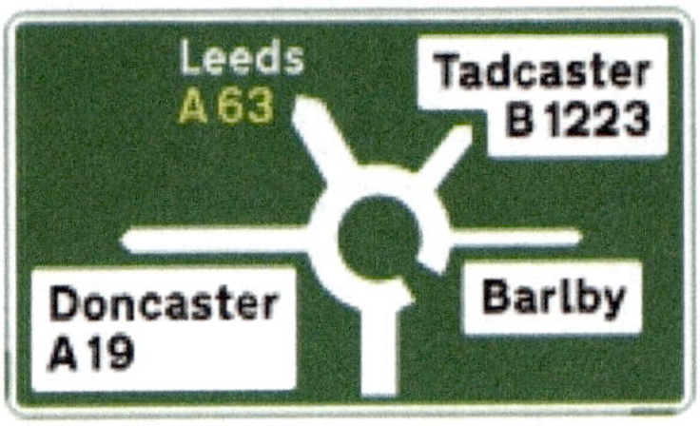

    - In addition, **simple roundabouts** are easier to observe, so there are no lane instructions, just a warning that you are approaching the roundabout.

- **Stop and Give Way Signs:**
    - **Stop Signs:** On your motorcycle, you must come to a complete stop at stop signs, just like any other road user.

    - **Give Way Signs:** Give way signs tell you to give way to traffic on the main road and are most commonly seen at roundabouts.

- **Prohibition and Warning Signs:** While riding your motorcycle, you may also see some prohibition and warning signs that motorcyclists should pay attention to, such as:
    - **No Solo Motorcycles:** When you see this, you cannot use your motorcycle on this road. Sometimes this warning may also be displayed with a time, meaning that you cannot use that road between those hours.
    - **Slippery Road:** These signs will warn you about road surfaces that may be slippery, usually due to rain, ice or oil.

    - **Loose Chippings:** This is one of the signs you may see while riding your motorcycle, usually in rural areas or roadworks. This is a warning sign that reminds you to be careful and slow down because of loose gravel or debris that can reduce your motorcycle's tyre grip.

There is too much to cover, but because of the subject matter of this book I have focused very little part of it. You can access the official source for all categorised traffic signs by scanning the QR code on the side.

Code: eb4a90

7.4 RIGHTS AND RESPONSIBILITIES OF MOTORCYCLISTS

As a motorcycle rider, it is vitally important that you understand your legal responsibilities and rights in the event of accidents, breakdowns and common scenarios you may encounter while riding.

7.4.1 LEGAL RESPONSIBILITIES

- **Insurance:** You must ensure that your motorcycle's insurance is valid and covers at least the legal minimum requirement of third party liability.

- **Vehicle Tax and MOT:** You will need to pay vehicle tax from the time your motorcycle is first purchased and will need to pass an MOT test after your motorcycle is three years old. Riding without a valid MOT or tax can result in a fine and points on your licence.

You can find more details about these topics in the previous **Chapter 6**.

7.4.2 IN CASE OF AN ACCIDENT

In case you are involved in an accident, sometimes it may not be easy to know what to do at that moment, you can handle this job calmly by keeping the following headings in mind.

- **Stop Safely:** It is legally obligatory to stop if you are involved in an accident, failure to do so is considered an offence and may result in a fine and points on your licence.

- **Exchange Details:** Everyone involved in an accident is required to provide their name, address and insurance details to the other parties involved. In cases of minor property damage, it is sufficient to exchange this information.

- **Report to the Police:** If as a result of the accident there are injuries, significant damages or if you were unable to provide your details at the time of the accident, for example if you hit a stopped vehicle and cannot find the person with whom you exchanged your details, you are legally obliged to report this to the police within 24 hours.

7.4.3 BREAKDOWN RESPONSIBILITIES

If your motorcycle breaks down, it can be dangerous, especially on motorways or busy roads, there are some things to look out for in these situations.

- **Move to Safety:** If possible, move your motorcycle to a safe area, such as an emergency lane or the side of the road.

- **Use Your Hazard Lights:** Switch on your hazard lights and wear your high-visibility vest if you have one. Stay off the road, especially if this happens to you on the motorway, stand behind the barriers and wait for help.

- **Breakdown Cover:** Having breakdown cover as part of your insurance or separately will save you a lot of hassle in this type of breakdown.

In this chapter, I have tried to share how you can achieve safe riding on your motorcycle by following the UK Highway Code, as well as some rules and tips specific to motorcycles. The information I have given here should be seen as a basic start to be aware of your responsibilities, respect traffic signs and always prioritise safety.

Code: 9c3564

For more detailed information on UK Highway Code, you can access detailed information from the official Highway Code using the QR code on the side.

8. MOTORCYCLE SAFETY AND RIDING ETIQUETTE

Motorcycling is an exciting activity, but it also carries significant risks if you are not careful. In this chapter, I will try to focus on basic safety practices and good riding habits to help you stay safe on the road on your motorcycle. It will be especially important to adapt your riding style to the unpredictable weather and changing road conditions in the UK and to always be aware of your surroundings.

8.1 THE IMPORTANCE OF DEFENSIVE RIDING

For motorcyclists, especially in the UK, defensive riding is one of the most vital skills you need to be able to use in the challenging conditions that frequent rain, slippery roads and urban areas present for motorcycling. Defensive riding allows you to recognise potential hazards in advance, anticipate them before they occur and be ready to react to the expected situation.

8.1.1 ANTICIPATING HAZARDS

- **Other Vehicles:** Always assume that the drivers of other vehicles cannot see your motorcycle. In particular, stay away from blind spots and avoid riding too close to large vehicles such as lorries, assuming that they cannot see you. Try to observe the behaviour of drivers in the traffic in front of you, and proceed with the assumption that drivers who make unexpected movements are more likely to make sudden lane changes or sudden braking.

- **Pedestrians:** In busy urban areas, pedestrians are likely to cross the road without warning, so be alert for pedestrians, especially around crossings, bus stops and parked cars, and try to adjust your speed accordingly.

- **Road Conditions:** Try to look out for potholes, gravel, oil leaks and uneven surfaces on UK roads, especially after heavy rain. Try as far as possible not to position yourself on the side of the road, as these hazards can quickly destabilise a motorcycle and cause an accident.

8.1.2 REACTING TO HAZARDS

- **Maintain a Safe Following Distance:** Especially in wet or icy conditions, always leave enough distance between you and the vehicle in front of you to avoid possible accidents in case of slipping when braking in emergency situations. You may not be riding a motorcycle when there is icing, but in low temperatures, humidity and precipitation, shaded areas or windy areas are prone to icing, especially try to be careful against black ice.

- **Use Your Horn and Lights:** Try to make yourself more visible on your motorcycle by using your horn or flashing your lights on and off in low visibility, or turn on your lights continuously to be more visible and to alert others of your presence.

- **Plan Escape Routes:** Always try to be aware of what is going on around you and it will be very useful for your safety to have a constant idea of where you can move to escape if an emergency situation arises.

8.2 ROAD POSITIONING

When riding your motorcycle, your position in the lane is of great importance for safe riding as it will determine how visible you are to other road users and how well you are able to react to obstacles.

8.2.1 URBAN RIDING

- **Positioning in Traffic:** To maximise your visibility to other drivers, ride in the centre of your lane, dominating the lane you are in. Try to avoid passing between cars as vehicles may suddenly change lanes and be alert to all possible traffic movements by adjusting your speed appropriately when filtering.

- **Approaching Junctions:** Always slow down when approaching junctions, as many accidents occur at junctions when vehicles exit unexpectedly or recklessly. Try to be in the most visible position from junctions and oncoming traffic.

8.2.2 RURAL RIDING

- **Country Roads:** While rural areas can be very pleasant for motorcycle riding, you are likely to encounter narrow roads, blind spots, debris and agricultural vehicles. As there is also wildlife in these areas, try to ride closer to the centre of your lane, depending on the road conditions, to react to such situations.

- **Blind Bends and Hill Crests**: Always reduce your speed when approaching a blind bend or hill, otherwise you may get into trouble from oncoming traffic or obstacles that may suddenly appear because you cannot see what is behind those points.

8.2.3 MOTORWAY RIDING

- **Lane Discipline:** Ride in the left lane unless overtaking, depending on weather and road conditions. Use your mirrors frequently, signal clearly before changing lanes and finally make the lane change with a life-saving (shoulder check) look.

- **Safe Distances:** It is always good to maintain a safe following distance. This distance will really help you in terms of your safety, especially since motorcycles are vehicles that are often not seen or paid attention to by other vehicle users.

8.3 CORNERING TECHNIQUES

Cornering on a motorcycle requires planning and precision, but it is also a skill that develops with practice. Whether you are riding on tight city bends or wide rural bends, maintaining control is the key to safe riding.

8.3.1 SLOW IN, FAST OUT

- **Approach Corners Slowly:** Always adjust your speed according to the corner before entering the bend, because slowing down while turning brings some risks. If you brake or cut speed during cornering, you may experience problems such as losing control of your motorcycle and slipping. Therefore, try to understand the structure of the bend in front of you by reading the road, paying attention to traffic signs and try to be at the appropriate speed for that bend before entering the bend.

- **Throttle Through the Exit:** When you enter a corner, generally ride at a constant speed appropriate to the corner to maintain balance and control, and when you see the exit of the corner, slowly increase the throttle and make the exit. You can easily embed this skill into your muscle memory by practising on most corners.

8.3.2 LOOK WHERE YOU WANT TO GO

- **Focus on the Exit Point:** There is a well-known saying, 'your motorcycle goes where you look', and this is indeed true in practice. If you focus on obstacles or the side of the road while riding your motorcycle, your motorcycle will tend to go there, which can drag you directly towards the obstacle or off the road. Therefore, you can ride more safely by focusing on the clear road you want to ride on at all times.

8.3.3 ADJUST FOR CONDITIONS

- **Wet or Icy Roads:** In general, it is important for your safety that you do not ride your motorcycle in weather that may be icy. However, if you have to use your motorcycle on wet or icy roads, reduce your speed even more than usual before entering bends and avoid sharp, sudden movements and acceleration that may cause loss of traction.

- **Gravel or Debris:** Gravel or leaves are very common on roads and bends, especially in rural areas. Since these can cause your tyres to lose grip when cornering rather than when going straight, slow down and try to be at a speed that will stand more upright in the corner.

8.4 GROUP RIDING ETIQUETTE

Especially riding with like-minded motorcycle riders is one of the most enjoyable experiences of motorcycling. However, clear communication and coordination within the group for group riding is very important for the safety of all riders in the group. In group riding, it is important to maintain appropriate distances and strong communication to avoid accidents.

8.4.1 COMMUNICATION SIGNALS

- **Hand Signals:** Especially if you are new to the riding group and there is no technological communication device between the group members, determine the hand signals for stopping, slowing down and indicating hazards by talking in advance. Thus, when everyone in the group knows the meaning of these signs and the places to use them, you will be riding more safely.

- **Mirrors:** Always check your mirrors to make sure that the motorcyclist behind you is still behind you and with the group. In this way, you can avoid breaking away from the group by adjusting your speed according to the group members who are behind at the traffic light or for any other reason.

8.4.2 MAINTAINING SPACING

- **Staggered Formation:** A staggered formation, especially in group rides, is one of the formations that should be preferred as it allows the group to move tightly compact while giving each rider more space to react to sudden changes.

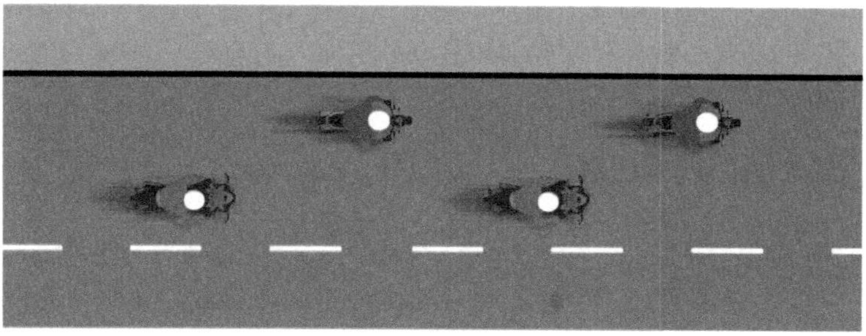

- **Safe Distance:** Try to maintain a safe following distance so that you can react in time to obstacles or changes in speed according to the situation and formation, whether in a staggered formation or not.

8.4.3 RIDING PACE

- **Ride at the Speed of the Slowest Rider:** Group rides will have motorcyclists of many different abilities, try to pace the group ride at a comfortable pace, especially one that the least experienced or slowest rider can handle.

- **Don't Overtake Recklessly:** In group rides, you will sometimes need to overtake when you are behind cars. However, unless it is really necessary and safe, try to avoid overtaking, especially in the group, and if you are going to overtake, try to do it in a controlled way and in a way that the riders in front and behind you can clearly understand.

8.5 RIDING IN NIGHT AND WEATHER CONDITIONS

The weather in the UK can be unpredictable even during the day before you set off, with frequent rain, fog and cold conditions during the day affecting visibility and handling. Adjusting your riding to these conditions is very important for your safety.

8.5.1 NIGHT RIDING

- **Use High-Visibility Gear:** First of all, remember that it is difficult for you to see others, others to see you at night, so try not to ride a motorcycle as much as possible. However, night riding may sometimes be inevitable and in these cases, try to take your precautions. Although some motorcycle clothing includes reflective materials, try to wear reflective clothing to achieve higher visibility and make sure that your motorcycle lights are working properly. On night journeys, try to ensure that other road users can see you both with your motorcycle lights and the clothing you are wearing.

- **Reduce Speed:** As visibility is poor when riding at night, travel at speeds that you consider safe, lower than you normally would, to give yourself more time to react to hazards.

8.5.2 RAINY CONDITIONS

- **Wet Roads:** The rain you will often encounter in the UK will reduce tyre grip and increase braking distances. In these conditions, try to ride more slowly and give yourself plenty of room to stop. Avoid sudden braking or acceleration and try not to lean your motorcycle too far into turns in case of skidding.

- **Puddles:** Be careful when riding your motorcycle as puddles, especially if the water is muddy, can hide potholes or other road hazards underneath.

8.5.3 FOG

- **Visibility:** Visibility will be extremely limited in foggy conditions, ride with your headlights and fog lights on if you have them. Switching on your high beams in foggy weather can sometimes reflect off the fog and reduce your visibility, so try to use low beams instead of high beams.

- **Increase Distance:** Always increase the distance between you and the vehicle in front of you in foggy weather, because the sudden braking of the vehicle in front of you due to low visibility can put you in trouble.

8.5.4 ICY AND SNOWY ROADS

- **Avoid Riding if Possible:** If the roads are icy or snowy, it is best to avoid riding altogether. If you must ride, go extremely slowly and try to avoid sudden movements, remembering that traction is severely lacking.

- **Pre-Ride Check:** Before setting off in winter weather, carefully check the tread and pressure of your tyres and make sure that your lights and signals are working properly.

8.5.5 WINDY CONDITIONS

- **Stay Light on the Controls:** Do not hold the handlebars of your motorcycle too tight in strong winds, keeping the controls light will prevent you from moving hard against the wind with a slight suspension effect with your arms against the wind.

- **Lean Into the Wind:** In crosswinds, especially if you are riding in areas such as viaducts and bridges that are very open to wind, lean slightly towards the wind to maintain balance. However, when passing through such places, you should be very careful according to the direction of the wind when passing by large vehicles such as large trucks and lorries. Because these vehicles will suddenly cut off the steady wind and make the wind come again suddenly after the vehicle passes. In these cases, you will also need to adjust the timing of your lean towards the wind well.

8.6 ADDITIONAL ESSENTIALS FOR MOTORCYCLE SAFETY

- **Wear Proper Gear Year-Round:** As the weather in the UK can change rapidly, wearing appropriate riding gear can help to stabilise the comfort of your ride throughout the day. You can maximise comfort by dressing in layers especially for these weather changes. Wearing lighter protective gear in the summer and waterproof, windproof, and thermal gear in the winter will help you be more comfortable throughout the year.

- **Regular Motorcycle Maintenance:** Regular checks of your tyres, lights, brakes and chain will keep your motorcycle in good condition and allow you to continue riding safely. Poorly maintained motorcycles will be much more likely to malfunction in adverse conditions.

- **Plan Your Route:** You can have a more comfortable and safer ride when you plan your route by checking the weather forecasts in the direction you will go before you set off, avoiding flooded areas or known roads with heavy traffic in bad weather.

In this chapter, I have tried to provide information on safe riding on UK roads according to weather and road conditions, as well as tactics to be considered in group riding and how to stay safer by applying defensive riding. Whether you are riding alone or with a group, this information will help you prepare to adapt to changing road, weather conditions and challenges.

9. COMMON MISTAKES NEW RIDERS MAKE AND HOW TO AVOID THEM

After passing an intensive motorcycle test programme, the freedom to ride a motorcycle is a real pleasure. However, there is also a high risk of mistakes that can be avoided with the right approach and precautions. Qualifying to ride a motorcycle will not immediately make you an experienced rider, it is important to learn from your mistakes and at the same time continue to practice to improve your skills in areas that you feel are difficult.

In this chapter, I will focus on common mistakes that new riders tend to make and try to give tips on how to avoid them and improve them in a good way.

9.1 OVERCONFIDENCE AFTER PASSING THE TEST

One of the most common pitfalls for new riders, even experienced riders who have just completed advanced training, is the surge of overconfidence after passing their test. While it is exciting to have the freedom and sense of achievement that comes with being validated with a motorcycle licence, this is actually a time to be cautious, especially at the very beginning.

Gaining riding experience is a gradual process that develops with time and practice, and overestimating your abilities can lead to mistakes. Here I will try to share the importance and benefits of staying humble, continuing to practice and keeping safety as the top priority.

9.1.1 THE LEARNING DOES NOT STOP

Passing the test is a great achievement and personal satisfaction, but remember that after passing the test you are only at the beginning of your adventure with the motorcycle. It is important for your development to continue to learn and challenge yourself through constant practice in different riding environments.

- **Tip:** *Practice, practice, practice... makes perfect.* You can improve your motorcycle experience by practising your motorcycle handling in different situations by riding in a variety of conditions, including rainy days, windy weather and busier times of the day. If you are a new rider, again knowing yourself and increasing the degree of difficulty according to you, riding against such situations will help you gain experience, gain self-confidence and improve your motorcycle riding.

- **Advanced Courses:** As a new rider, the best investment you can make in your safety is continuous training and practice. Post-test advanced training courses such as **IAM RoadSmart** or **RoSPA** (more details in **Chapter 10**) will help you improve your technique, road awareness and defensive riding skills, helping you to become a smooth and safe rider.

- **Riding with an Experienced Partner:** Riding with a more experienced friend or mentor will be incredibly beneficial. Although your friend or mentor may not be an instructor, they can pass on their experience and help you in some areas where you need to improve. Just make sure that this is a constructive person who respects your skill level and doesn't pressure you to take unnecessary risks.

9.1.2 STAY HUMBLE ON THE ROAD

New motorcycle riders try to push their limits by trying to catch up with faster riders by riding beyond their skill level. However, whether you are a new or experienced motorcycle rider on the road, having a modest attitude and continuing to ride in accordance with your riding skills will improve your self-confidence and make you safe.

- **Avoid Showing Off:** It is natural to be proud of your skills after getting your motorcycle licence, but it is important for your safety that you always try to ride within your current experience. Avoid showing off by riding above your skill, especially to catch up with more experienced riders. Remember, it is never a problem to ride at your own pace, especially if you are in a group ride, try to focus on your own riding, not the speed of others.

- **Control Your Speed:** Overconfidence often leads to uncontrolled speeding, which can reduce your reaction time and make it more difficult to deal with unexpected hazards. Observe speed limits, especially in areas with heavy traffic and pedestrians. Experienced riders make a habit of adjusting their speed according to visibility, road quality and traffic flow to ensure safer riding, so follow these methods and keep your speed within the limits.

- **Tip:** It is one of the most important points to realise riding by knowing your limits. It is natural to feel uncomfortable riding in difficult conditions or on routes where you do not feel comfortable yet, and these will improve as your experience increases as you practice. Most importantly, focus on improving your skills without feeling additional pressure, while riding at the near upper limits of your comfort zone to enhance your experience.

9.1.3 BUILDING REAL-WORLD RIDING EXPERIENCE

Overconfidence comes from underestimating or failing to anticipate the real-world challenges that can arise, especially in everyday riding. Always improving your experience as much as possible under a variety of roads and conditions will help you overcome any unfavourable situations you encounter in such conditions.

- **Vary Your Routes:** Focus on improving your riding in changing traffic conditions on different routes, rather than just the routes you know and have always travelled. As you will face different scenarios on each different route, this will help our experiment to improve in these conditions.

- **Ride in Different Conditions:** Although it is not preferred to ride in rainy weather, night and heavy traffic hours, it is one of the situations you will encounter. When you encounter these situations, plan to ride to increase your experience in such weather so that you can ride safely and confidently. These rides will improve your ability and make you more prepared for unexpected conditions. For example, wet roads will affect braking and turning, while night riding will give you experience in focusing on road signs and lighting and controlling your speed according to these conditions.

- **Practice Common Manoeuvres:** Repeatedly practising basic manoeuvres such as U-turns, emergency stops and hazard avoidance in parking areas off public roads at regular intervals will help develop your muscle memory. Most of these manoeuvres are ones that you will need in your everyday traffic riding.

9.1.4 SELF-ASSESSMENT AND REFLECTION

Thinking about your riding after every ride will be a powerful tool for further improving your riding. This is one of the most important development tracking methods, especially in advanced riding training.

- **Keep a Riding Journal:** You may have struggled with a turn or you may have had a close call, taking note of these after the ride will help you track your progress and identify areas where you need to practice later. After each ride is over, you can take note of these situations, as well as the situations that went well, and take out the practices that you will be good to do for the next rides, so you can continue your development in a controlled manner. You can use Motorcycle Ride Journal Book by scanning the QR code.

Code: 65d7d7

- **Evaluate Your Confidence Levels:** Feelings such as taking excessive risks or not being able to tolerate slower drivers can actually be seen as signs of overconfidence. Since these types of feelings are behaviours that can be a problem for your safety from time to time, by reminding yourself of them, you can suggest yourself and motivate yourself to ride more safely.

- **Focus on Improvement, Not Perfection:** You should remember that even experienced riders always have room for improvement. Improving your skills step by step instead of striving for perfection will reduce the pressure and ensure gradual and sustainable improvement.

9.2 INADEQUATE GEAR

Many new riders may tend to underestimate the importance of quality riding equipment, focusing more on the motorbike and its cost. Of course budget considerations are an important factor, but the safety of your personal equipment should be one of the most important investment items in motorcycling. Good equipment does not always mean expensive equipment, nor does it mean that every equipment will be comfortable. I will try to give information on important issues that should be considered when choosing motorcycle riding equipment.

9.2.1 INVEST IN SAFETY

As people who use motorcycles, of course, we may also be attracted to the visual appeal of the motorcycle. Here, it is quite natural that you want the equipment choices to match our motorcycle in terms of style and provide a visual integrity. However, you should remember that in the event of an accident, it is not the style of your equipment that protects you from serious injuries, but how safe your equipment is. Here I will try to explain both compulsory and non-compulsory but important riding equipment for your safety and give some tips.

- **Helmet:** Helmet is the most important and mandatory piece of motorcycle safety equipment. Choosing a good helmet will make the difference between life and death in serious accidents as well as providing protection against head injuries.

    - **What to Look For:** Examine the helmets evaluated by the SHARP organisation in the UK. The **SHARP rating system**, created by the UK Department for Transport, aims to assign a safety rating between one and five stars by evaluating helmets according to impact tests.

    - **Type and Fit:** I shared the details of different types of helmets in detail in **Chapter 5**. Here, especially according to the shape of your head and face, the helmet that provides a tight and comfortable fit without any pressure points on your head and face will be the helmet model you need to prefer.

    - **Tip:** Budget is important, but don't sacrifice helmet quality for price alone. Even a mid-range helmet rated well by Sharp can provide much more protection than a more cheaper helmet. However, it would not be correct to conclude that every full-face helmet is reliable, it will be useful to examine the Sharp test results specific to the helmet you are considering buying.

- **Jacket and Gloves:** Riding jackets and gloves are designed with protective armour and abrasion-resistant materials to protect your hands, arms, legs, hips, which will be the first contact after your head in case of any accident, fall and skid. Jackets and gloves are not legally mandatory, but they are important equipment that you should use for your safety.

- **Jackets:** It is important that jackets have **CE approved armour**, especially in the elbow, shoulder and back areas, at least it is important to have pockets that can attach armour to these areas even if the jacket does not come with armour. Thus, you can make it safe by making these additions to your jacket after purchase. Leather and high quality textile materials are ideal materials both in terms of abrasion resistance and comfort. Brands such as **Dainese**, **Alpinestars**, **Rukka** and **Richa** are some popular brands that we can count with reliable protective equipment.

- **Gloves:** Gloves have an important function in protecting our hands, which are perhaps the most neglected but one of our limbs that will be damaged in the slightest fall even where you are not moving. When choosing gloves, choose gloves that provide impact protection with reinforced knuckles, palms and wrists. At the same time, make sure that it fits well on your hand so that you can properly access the controls on your handlebars. Otherwise, even if your glove has good protection, it may jeopardise your safety by causing you problems with motorcycle controls because you do not master the controls.

- **Boots:** Feet are a particularly vulnerable part of your body in the event of an accident or even if you drop the motorcycle from a standstill, so boots are essential for foot and ankle protection.

- **Features:** Look for ankle-length or taller style boots with reinforced ankles, sturdy soles and protective toes, which will provide more protection than low-cut shoes.

- **Tip:** Avoid riding a motorcycle in normal shoes or trainers, as they will not protect your feet in the event of an accident and can cause serious injury to your feet.

9.2.2 WEATHER-APPROPRIATE GEAR

The fact that weather conditions in the UK are constantly changing even during the day can make it difficult to decide on the equipment suitable for these conditions. However, if you do not choose equipment to cover the weather possibilities that will be experienced that day, the conditions you will encounter may cause you to be distracted while riding, weaken your control and even hypothermia in extreme cases.

- **Layered Clothing:** In particular, the most appropriate method of adapting to changing weather conditions is to adapt to different temperatures by choosing layered clothing, adding or removing layers as needed. A moisture-wicking base layer will help regulate body temperature, while a thermal layer will provide warmth in colder weather. For example, when the weather warms up in the afternoon, you can still ride comfortably by taking off the thermal layer you wore in the morning when it was cold.

- **Waterproofing:** Riding in the rain can be uncomfortable and dangerous if your equipment is not waterproof, especially when riding in the UK. Wet clothes not only cause discomfort, but this discomfort can also jeopardise your safety as it will indirectly affect your riding.

- **Gore-Tex and Other Waterproof Fabrics:** There are many material brands such as Gore-Tex, Drystar, D-Dry, H2Out, which add waterproof properties among motorcycle gear equipment. You can see the names of these materials in many products, these materials provide waterproof properties to products such as jackets, gloves, trousers, boots. In this respect, it will be useful to read comments and reviews while evaluating the price performance of the product you will prefer. Textile garments with high breathability and waterproof properties such as Gore-Tex will be popular choices that keep comfort high in general.

- **Rain Suits:** Many riders keep a compact rain jacket in their bag or rucksack, even if their own clothing is not waterproof. This lightweight, waterproof outer layer can be worn over normal motorcycle clothing when caught in the rain, helping you to avoid getting wet in the rain.

- **Ventilation:** Apart from rain and cold, another effective situation is hot weather. Choosing jackets and trousers with ventilation panels for hot weather will help you to continue riding comfortably in hot weather. Apart from this, jackets with summer mesh panels that are more suitable for hot weather will be very helpful in ventilation. However, it will be good for your safety to focus on models that you can wear protection in mesh jackets.

9.2.3 CHOOSING THE RIGHT FIT AND STYLE

Even if you buy the best equipment in the world, if it doesn't fit you correctly, it can slip during an accident and reduce its effectiveness, which will have unpleasant consequences. Therefore, choosing equipment in sizes that do not fit you just for style or comfort may cause you trouble in unexpected situations.

- **Helmet Fit:** The discomfort of your helmet is one of the most undesirable situations for a motorcyclist while riding. However, buying a little loose one, not tight, will also jeopardise your safety. The best way to find the most suitable helmet for you by trying different brands and models according to your head shape and size. Try to find a helmet that is both comfortable but fits snugly, especially without pressure points on your head and at the same time you will not put a finger between your forehead and helmet to test tightness.

- **Jacket Fit:** The jackets you will use for motorcycle riding should be tight enough to hold the armour that comes with it or that you have added later, but should not restrict your arm movements to easily control the motorcycle.

- **Boots Fit:** Choose boots that fit tightly around your ankles and have the flexibility to allow gear changes while riding the motorcycle and have extra protection on the toes and ankles. Especially sports shoes and shoes that do not wrap the ankles may make you look good for walking, but this can cause you a lot of trouble in the event of an accident on the motorcycle.

Tip: Take the time to try different brands and models to find the combination that fits your body best, is safe and provides your comfort needs. The right equipment should feel like a second skin but should not be restrictive.

9.2.4 CE RATINGS, AAA CLASSES, AND PROTECTION STANDARDS

When selecting your safety equipment, you should consider not only the equipment's design but also additional classifications like CE (Conformité Européenne) ratings and AAA safety standards in the UK and Europe. These ratings and classifications generally indicate the levels of protection provided against abrasion, impact and wear during a collision.

CE Ratings for Armour

Motorcycle protective equipment usually includes either built-in or removable CE rated armour. If the equipment you are interested in does not have any armour, check that it has pockets that can be fitted with armour and do not give much preference to equipment that cannot be fitted with armour. These CE ratings assess the impact protection of critical areas such as elbows, shoulders, knees and hips. They are divided into two levels:

- **Level 1:** Equipment that provides basic protection and is suitable for urban or short-distance riding. They are generally thinner and more flexible, when you ride in the city and short distance, equipment with this rating can generally meet your needs. It is comfortable because of its high flexibility, but it should not be forgotten that this level of protection also has limits. The maximum transmitted force during impact tests is **35 kN (kilonewton)** for these armours.

- **Level 2:** Slightly bulkier than Level 1 armour, it absorbs higher impact forces and is recommended for long distance or higher speed riding. However, it may not be correct to restrict it only to these rides. In this respect, it would be appropriate to choose your level by getting to know yourself and considering which one is more suitable for your motorcycle riding. The maximum transmitted force during impact tests is **20 kN (kilonewton)** for these armours.

Tip: When purchasing equipment, it is worth checking the CE labelling inside the jacket or trousers to verify these levels of protection.

CE EN 17092 Classification for Clothing

Since 2018, motorcycle clothing sold in the UK and Europe must comply with the CE EN 17092 standard. Since these standards were not a requirement before this date, it will be useful to consider them when you buy second-hand clothing. According to abrasion resistance, tear strength and seam integrity, the CE EN 17092 standard is divided into five categories:

- **AAA (High Protection):** AAA, the highest level of abrasion resistance according to the standards, is particularly suitable for high-speed riding, long tours and track use. It is more common in leather clothing, but is also common in high-end textile equipment.

- **AA (Medium Protection):** This category provides protection that balances protection and comfort, ideal for touring and everyday riding.

- **A (Basic Protection):** This category focuses on comfort with lighter materials. These levels are common in summer clothing and are designed for urban and everyday riders.

- **B (Abrasion Protection Only):** This class is similar to A, but without built-in impact protectors. In this case they are designed to provide abrasion protection only. In this case, you can additionally increase safety with independent body armour.

- **C (Impact Protection Only):** This is the least protective class and includes protective underwear or individual pieces of armour for certain body parts that are impact resistant but not abrasion resistant.

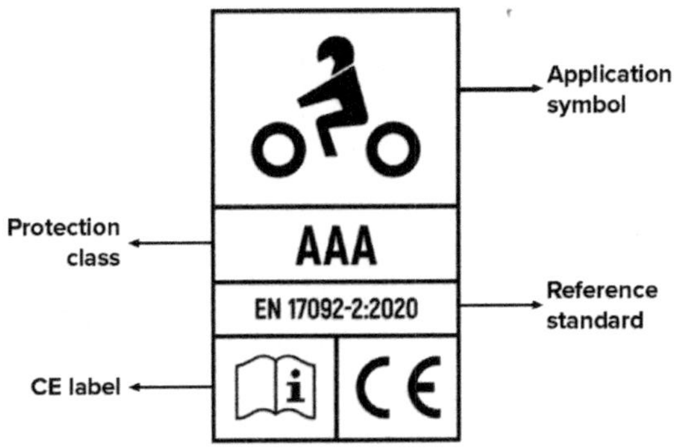

Tip: For maximum safety at least AA-rated clothing will be suitable, but for touring or high-speed rides try to choose AAA-rated equipment. You can see an example label above of AAA class image with explanation of the sections.

Additional Safety Standards

In addition to CE ratings, there are other certifications to consider when choosing your equipment:

- **EN 13595 (Older Standard):** This old standard has been replaced by the current standard EN 17092 and you should prefer these new products. However, considering that there is also second-hand sales, especially in motorcycle clothing, it may also be useful to look for the EN 13595 label, which focuses on standard abrasion, impact and explosion resistance in old products.

- **UKCA Marking:** It is necessary to disperse some confusion about UKCA marking. UKCA was introduced after Brexit as the British equivalent of the European CE marking to certify compliance with safety standards for many different products, including motorcycle clothing. Initially, the UK government made UKCA certification mandatory for products sold in the UK from January 2022, with UKCA labelling becoming mandatory from January 2023.

  However, despite significant investment by manufacturers, this deadline was repeatedly postponed and finally the decision was taken in August 2023 to allow **CE marking to be accepted indefinitely in the UK**. Since then UKCA certification has become optional and applies mainly only to sales in the UK, whereas CE certification can be sold to both the UK and European markets.

Key Features to Look For

- **Abrasion Resistance:** While leather garments generally offer superior abrasion resistance compared to textiles, textiles reinforced with materials such as Kevlar, Cordura or Aramid fibres are also popular for abrasion resistance.

- **Impact Absorption:** Make sure that your suit's armour placement covers vulnerable areas such as elbows, shoulders, knees, hips and back. You may also want to consider a chest protector to increase your safety further.

- **Seam Strength:** Models with double or triple stitched seams that reduce the chance of tearing during slipping will be beneficial in terms of safety, as they ensure that the fabric does not fall apart for longer duration.

- **Fit and Comfort:** As I mentioned before, it is important that the armour is in the right places, just like the clothes that fit you perfectly, it ensures that the armour stays in place to protect the right place during an impact. So try on more than one size and brand to find the best fit for your body type.

9.2.5 BUDGET-FRIENDLY OPTIONS WITHOUT COMPROMISING SAFETY

Everyone probably wants to buy high quality motorcycle equipment, but high quality equipment is often expensive and not always affordable. So here are some budget-friendly tips for choosing equipment.

- **Prioritise Key Items:** Especially if you're on a tight budget, you can proceed with a gradual prioritisation. Invest in a high-quality helmet and jacket first, then try to invest in gloves and boots as soon as possible.

- **Buy Second-Hand:** You can consider buying lightly used equipment from trusted sources, but I do not recommend buying used helmets. Because helmets are delicate, always buy new helmets as they cannot be guaranteed to continue to maintain their durability.

- **Look for Sales and Outlet Deals:** Many reputable brands occasionally offer discounts on previous season models. Keep an eye out for sales at local motorcycle shops or online retailers to find high-quality equipment at a lower price.

9.3 IGNORING MAINTENANCE

Many new riders, especially if they own a new motorcycle, may ignore routine maintenance, assuming that their motorcycle will run smoothly without regular maintenance. However, neglecting maintenance can result in unexpected breakdowns, costly repairs and safety risks.

9.3.1 ROUTINE CHECKS

By getting into the habit of performing routine checks on your motorcycle, you can easily prevent problems on the road. Most of these checks do not require mechanical expertise, thanks to these simple checks, you can keep your motorcycle's performance and safety at the highest level by recognising the problems of your motorcycle in advance.

- **Oil Level:** Check your motorcycle's oil level before each ride or at least once a week. Low oil levels can cause engine wear and overheating. To check the oil, you can check the dipstick on your motorcycle or the oil indicator glass on recent new motorcycles.

- **Tyre Pressure and Tread:** Your tyres are the only point of contact with the ground when your motorcycle is in motion, and their proper condition is critical for braking and fuel efficiency. Under- or over-inflated tyres can adversely affect grip, so you should check both tyres regularly with a tyre pressure gauge, especially before every long ride. Tyre tread depth should also be checked regularly, as worn tyres can pose a safety risk as they reduce traction, especially in wet weather.

- **Chain Tension and Lubrication:** A loose chain can slip and become dislodged, whereas a tight or dry chain can break and pose a serious safety risk. Lubricate the chain regularly and adjust the tension according to your motorcycle's manual. In this way, you can extend the life of your chain and save yourself from possible chain-related problems while riding.

- **Brake Fluid and Pads:** Check brake fluid levels regularly and add or replace as necessary. Also check your brake pads for wear and replace them when they become too thin, as worn brake pads can increase stopping distance.

- **Tool Bag:** Carrying a small tool kit on your motorcycle will help you make adjustments when needed on the road. At the same time, do not forget to add the appropriate fuses for your motorcycle in this toolbox, these small fuses can be life-saver, as there may be fuse blowing situations on the road.

Tip: Create a simple checklist for these routine checks and review it especially before long rides. I have mentioned the topics have briefly summarised here in more detail in **Chapter 5**, reading those sections again in detail will help you to have a full command of the subject.

9.3.2 SCHEDULE REGULAR SERVICING

In order to ensure that your motorcycle runs smoothly, apart from your regular checks, more detailed and periodic maintenance by a professional mechanic will ensure that potential problems on your motorcycle are recognised early, solutions are produced and it will continue to run smoothly.

- **Brake Checks and Oil Changes:** Regular maintenance includes oil changes, brake checks and some checks that can prevent major problems. A mechanic will also top up or replace any missing fluids and making sure everything is in working order, inspect hoses and return the motorcycle to you in good condition.

- **Valve Adjustments and Chain Replacement:** A well-maintained chain and proper valve adjustment will contribute to smooth shifting and optimum engine performance for your motorcycle. Adjusting or replacing these components of your motorcycle over time will help you maintain this performance for a long time.

Tip: Your motorcycle manufacturer will recommend certain service intervals for your motorcycle model. This is usually planned for current new motorcycles as they reach a certain mileage, or annually if you have not reached that mileage within that year. Keeping a record of your motorcycle's service history in the service booklet provided for you to keep the service history of your motorcycle every time you go to the service will help the resale value and remind you of when you have been serviced.

9.4 POOR ROAD AWARENESS

Assuming that other drivers do not always see you, you should adjust your riding and awareness accordingly. Staying alert, defensive, being proactive and expecting the unexpected will significantly increase your safety.

9.4.1 ANTICIPATING OTHER ROAD USERS

Assuming that other drivers haven't seen you is a useful mindset for staying alert and defensive. Being proactive and expecting the unexpected can significantly improve your safety.

- **Defensive Riding:** Keep a safe distance from other vehicles, especially large ones, and avoid their blind spots. Large vehicles such as lorries and buses often have low visibility and may not see you, so stay alert and position yourself where you are most visible on the road.

- **Anticipate Road Hazards:** Continuously scanning the road ahead of you will help you recognise sudden lane changes, road debris and pedestrian crossings ahead of you and help you avoid potential hazards. While doing this, it will also allow you to frequently follow what is happening in the traffic behind you with your mirrors and take timing and position accordingly.

Tip: Practicing defensive techniques such as thinking of a virtual "safety bubble" distance around your motorcycle and planning continuous escape routes in case you need to swerve or brake suddenly will benefit your safety.

9.4.2 SHOULDER CHECKS (CRITICAL SAFETY TIP)

It is vital for a new rider to perform a proper shoulder check, also known as a **life saver**, which is often overlooked but should become a habit. Shoulder checks are a very important check to ensure you are aware of vehicles in your blind spots when changing lanes or turning.

- **When to Perform Shoulder Checks:** Before changing lanes, overtaking or turning, always check over your shoulder for traffic to your side and rear. Even with mirrors, a shoulder check will ensure that there is nothing hidden in your blind spot.

- **Making it a Habit:** It's easy to rely on mirrors, but relying on a mirror alone in a confined space can cause you to miss important details with serious consequences. To make this basic skill a habit, it helps to practice shoulder checks frequently, even in low traffic conditions.

Tip: Practise shoulder checks on your rides until they become second nature, as this practice will help you avoid collisions and increase your overall road awareness.

9.5 BAD HABITS

Sometimes bad habits can get in the way of being a skilful rider who prioritises safety. Recognising and correcting these habits will help you become a confident motorcyclist.

9.5.1 FORGETTING TO CANCEL INDICATORS

The turn signals on most motorcycles are usually not automatically cancelled as in current cars. Without automatic cancellation, it's easy to forget them, which can confuse other road users and cause problems.

- **Make it a Habit:** After every turn or lane change, check to see if your signals are still on. Try to get into the habit of looking at the signal indicator when straightening after a turn.

Tip: It is helpful to get into the habit of checking your signals every few seconds until you are sure they have been cancelled. You can also start to get into the habit of pressing the signal cancellation button once or twice after each turn.

9.5.2 POOR LANE DISCIPLINE

Good lane discipline will not only improve your safety on the road, it will also make you more predictable to other drivers. In addition, frequent lane changes and weaving between cars will increase your risk of an accident.

- **Stay in Your Lane:** Stay in your lane as much as possible and only change lanes when necessary. Position yourself to dominate the lane to maximise the visibility to other road users.

- **Filtering:** Although it is legal to filter in slow moving traffic in the UK, always watch out for vehicles that may suddenly change lanes or open doors without warning.

9.5.3 IMPROPER USE OF THE FRONT AND REAR BRAKES

It is a common mistake for new riders to rely solely on the front or rear brake, or even the habit of using the rear brake instead of the front brake. Mastering a balanced use of the front and rear brake will help you to be in control of braking, especially in emergency situations.

- **Balanced Braking:** Use both brakes together, with gradual more pressure on the front brake and light gradual application of the rear brake. This method will provide a balanced stop without locking the wheels, especially in wet or slippery conditions.

- **Practice Emergency Stops:** Regularly practising emergency stops in safe and traffic-free areas will help to embed balanced braking into muscle memory. The more comfortable you are with controlling your brakes, the more controlled and safe your stops will be.

9.6 RIDING IN ADVERSE WEATHER CONDITIONS

The UK's unpredictable weather conditions mean that you cannot escape riding in rain, fog and cold. Failure to adjust your riding style to these unfavourable conditions can lead to serious accidents.

9.6.1 WET ROADS AND REDUCED TRACTION

The reduced traction in wet weather can cause you to lose control, so you need to be extra careful.

- **Adjust Your Speed:** Slow down in wet weather conditions as braking distances are long and the risk of skidding is high. For acceleration, braking and cornering, try to take your actions with softer, gradual movements, not sudden.

- **Avoid Slippery Surfaces:** Painted road markings, metal gratings and manhole covers are areas that become slippery when wet and pose a serious danger. Sometimes you cannot avoid these surfaces while riding, but in general, avoid them if possible or cross them with a minimum angle to reduce the chance of slipping.

Tip: Always make sure that your tyres have adequate tread depth and the appropriate pressure, as this is a primary requirement for better grip in wet conditions.

9.6.2 VISIBILITY IN RAIN AND FOG

You may be less apparent and run the danger of getting into an accident in rain and fog since both you and other drivers will have very poor vision.

- **High-Visibility Gear:** Invest in high visibility or reflective clothing to increase your visibility in bad weather. Reflective strips on your jacket or helmet can make a big difference as they provide extra visibility.

- **Ensure Light Functionality:** Regularly check that your lights are clean and working well, as the visibility of lights can be reduced by dirt and moisture in such weather. Try to use low beams to avoid reflections and glare, especially in foggy weather.

Tip: To improve the visibility of your motorcycle in adverse conditions, you may want to consider adding temporary auxiliary lights, which will help other drivers to see you more easily. As it may not be legal to permanently attach these to your motorcycle, you may instead want to consider applying them on yourself or on bags, which are more likely to be temporary.

In this chapter I have tried to show that becoming a skilful motorcyclist takes time, practice and patience, and that common mistakes new riders make and what to do to develop better, safer riding habits in general. Try to continually improve these skills and become a safer rider as you ride your motorcycle on the road.

10. ADVANCED MOTORCYCLE RIDING SKILLS AND TRAINING OPTIONS

After passing your motorcycle exams and getting your licence, you should not think that your learning process ends here. Riding a motorcycle safely and confidently is a lifelong learning process. If you want to become a more defensive rider, gain confidence or improve your off-road skills, in this section I will try to focus on post-licence training and riding options that will take your skills to the next level.

10.1 ADVANCED RIDING COURSES

Advanced riding courses aim to help motorcyclists improve their skills, increase safety awareness and gain confidence in complex riding situations, whether you are a new rider or an experienced rider. These courses go beyond basic training and focus on equipping you with advanced techniques such as road safety and hazard prediction. Two of the most popular advanced riding options in the UK are **IAM RoadSmart** and **RoSPA**. Both provide valuable training that can improve your motorcycle riding skills and even reduce your motorcycle insurance premiums with some insurance companies.

10.1.1 IAM ROADSMART ADVANCED RIDER COURSE

The **Institute of Advanced Motorists (IAM) RoadSmart** is one of the leading organisations in the UK offering a structured advanced motorcycle training course to improve riding techniques and decision making skills. The course is built around the **IPSGA** motorcycle control system, a method used in police rider training to promote a systematic, defensive and effective riding style.

- **Course Structure:** The IAM RoadSmart course involves a series of observed rides conducted one-to-one with an experienced, IAM accredited observer. The observers endeavour to provide constructive feedback and guidance by stopping at regular intervals during each ride and sitting with you at the end of the ride to evaluate the ride. The **IPSGA system** on which the course is based comprises the following topics:
    - **(I)nformation:** Gathering information about the road, conditions and other road users and using it in your riding to plan your next move.
    - **(P)osition:** Placing your motorcycle in the safest and most visible position to road users for approaching hazards and manoeuvres.
    - **(S)peed:** Continuously adjusting your speed to suit the situation and road conditions.
    - **(G)ear:** Selecting the correct gear for maximum control and efficiency.
    - **(A)cceleration:** Accelerating smoothly and safely to maintain stability and control.

- **Skills Covered Using IPSGA**

  The course focuses on improving your riding to cope with real world situations using IPSGA principles, and will give you the chance to learn and apply them:

  - **Positioning for Safety and Visibility:** You will learn how to ride your motorcycle with the best possible view of the road ahead, while maintaining a position that maximises your visibility to others.

  - **Hazard Anticipation and Observation:** While effectively scanning the road with your eyes, you will learn to anticipate the actions of other road users using the "Information" phase of the IPSGA.

  - **Precise Speed and Gear Selection:** You will learn how to smoothly adjust speed and select the appropriate gear in the 'Speed' and 'Gear' stages before hazards or bends.

  - **Turning and Overtaking:** You will develop the ability to balance safety with skill by applying systematic control in turning and overtaking.

  - **Soft Acceleration and Braking:** You will develop advanced techniques for accelerating and braking smoothly while maintaining traction and stability.

- **Certification:** On completing the course, riders undergo an assessment. Passing this qualifies riders for IAM certification, which is recognised as a mark of advanced competency. IAM certification can sometimes reduce insurance premiums as insurers view IAM-trained riders as lower-risk.

- **Tips for Success:**
  - **Practice Between Sessions:** You will need to practise regularly so that the IPSGA system you apply while riding with an observer becomes second nature. Ride often, especially focusing on the notes taken by the observer as a result of the observation, and try to apply the techniques you have learnt.
  - **Be Open to Feedback:** Observers are there to guide you, not to criticise you. Try to internalise the constructive feedback of the observers, you will start to see its contribution to your riding.
  - **Elevate Your Riding with IPSGA:** Focus on consistently applying the IPSGA principles, which will improve your ability to ride more safely and predictably in a variety of road conditions.

10.1.2 ROSPA ADVANCED RIDERS COURSE

The **Royal Society for the Prevention of Accidents (RoSPA)** is an advanced motorcycle course whose main aim is to emphasise accident prevention, safety and hazard awareness in a wide range of riding scenarios.

- **Course Focus:** RoSPA's training concentrates on defensive riding techniques, hazard recognition and accident prevention. It also incorporates elements of **road-craft** that help riders make safer decisions by focusing on forward planning and observation skills.

- **Grading System:** RoSPA grades riders as Bronze, Silver or Gold based on their performance in the final test taken at the end of RoSPA. The RoSPA Gold standard is recognised as the highest civilian motorcycle qualification in the UK. RoSPA recommends re-testing every three years to keep skills up to date to the RoSPA standard in case acquired skills are subject to changes in road environments or personal habits.
- **Skills Covered:**
    - **Road Positioning and Anticipation:** While riding motorcycles, you will learn where and how to position yourself on the road for maximum safety and efficiency.
    - **Advanced Cornering and Acceleration Control:** You will develop the ability to apply smoother acceleration, braking and cornering techniques to deal with challenging road conditions.
    - **Risk Management:** Identify and assess the risks in a variety of road scenarios, from city streets to rural routes, and improve how to plan your riding approach accordingly.
- **Certification and Benefits:** Regular re-tests will help you stay up to date with best practice. Some insurance companies recognise RoSPA certification and can offer discounts on motorcycle insurance.

Tip: Both IAM RoadSmart and RoSPA courses will provide a significant return on investment, both personally and financially. By taking such advanced courses, you cannot only improve your practical riding skills and hazard awareness, but also benefit financially in the long term by reducing insurance premiums.

10.1.3 OTHER ADVANCED RIDING COURSES IN THE UK

I have already shared in detail the most popular advanced riding courses in the UK, IAM RoadSmart and RoSPA, but advanced riding courses in the UK are not limited to these. I will briefly mention a few popular advanced riding courses, each offering unique training benefits:

- **BikeSafe:** This initiative is run by police forces across the UK. BikeSafe aims to provide motorcyclists with workshops covering observation, hazard awareness, cornering and road positioning. The course takes place over one day, usually involving a classroom session followed by an observed ride with police motorcyclists. Although no certificate is offered at the end of this course, it is recommended as a starting point for riders new to advanced rider training.

- **Enhanced Rider Scheme (ERS):** Developed by the Driver and Vehicle Standards Agency (DVSA), the Enhanced Rider Scheme is designed to cover topics such as cornering, braking and managing heavy traffic for riders who have completed their basic training, or who have taken a break from motorcycling and are returning, and for riders who want to improve their skills without a final test. Riders receive an ERS certificate on completion of the course and this can be used for discounts with some insurance companies.

- **BMW Motorrad Rider Training:** Run by BMW, this course offers advanced courses alongside regular motorcycle riding licence courses for all riders, regardless of motorcycle brand. The advanced training also focuses on road positioning, emergency braking and cornering skills. The course offers courses that appeal to many different motorcycle riders, such as personalised one-to-one training, special training for returning riders after a long break, accelerated advanced courses.

- **California Superbike School (CSS):** The California Superbike School offers on-track training that significantly improves motorcycle handling, cornering and throttle control. The techniques learnt here can be applied to road riding, especially for riders who want to improve control and stability at higher speeds. The CSS is especially ideal for those who are interested in track days or want to improve their technical road handling skills in a controlled off-traffic area.

Tip: Each of these courses has its own advantages, so you can choose the course that suits you best by identifying your own needs, whether they are safety-orientated, performance-orientated or simply skills development.

10.2 TRACK DAYS

If you want to get to know your motorcycle better in a controlled and safe environment and develop your own skills in a controlled area, **track days** are a very suitable activity for this. You can participate in a track day so that you can fully focus on your motorcycle and your riding without worrying about traffic, pedestrians or road hazards, especially skills where it is not legal and unsafe to ride at high speed on public roads. Track days can help accelerate and develop basic riding skills such as road positioning, speed and braking.

10.2.1 WHAT TO EXPECT ON A TRACK DAY

- **Track Day Basics:** A track day allows you to ride timed on a professional race track, usually with other riders. These events are not intended for racing, but are practice sessions aimed at helping you develop specific riding techniques such as cornering, braking and setting your speed smoothly through corners. Depending on the circuit you are travelling to, you can find a session suitable for all levels of rider on track days, with some circuits also offering beginner sessions and coaching.

- **Safety Precautions:** Due to the nature of track days, safety is a top priority. Before starting each event, you must attend a mandatory safety briefing covering track rules, riding etiquette and emergency procedures. Marshals are stationed around the track to monitor riders and respond to any incidents. As safety is at the forefront of these rides, in addition, full protective equipment is usually required, such as a helmet, gloves, one piece of leather (or two pieces of leather fastened together with a zip) and ankle-covering boots. Your motorcycle will need to undergo a basic safety inspection, including checks for tyres, brakes and fluid leaks, to determine if it is suitable for the track.

- **Motorcycle Preparation:** Some tracks may require you to remove or tape mirrors to minimise distractions. As you will need to ensure that your motorcycle is in good mechanical condition, check tyre pressure and fuel levels, and you may also want to consider using tyres specifically designed for high-speed riding if possible. Many circuits also impose certain noise limits, so you will need to make sure that the motorcycle you are using can cope with these.

- **Skill Development:** Track days help you practise techniques that are not safe on public roads, such as leaning more in corners, accelerating more aggressively and braking at higher speeds. Track days will especially help you gain better throttle control, sharper reflexes and a better understanding of how your motorcycle reacts in different situations. Track riding will also help improve your muscle memory with repeated practice on the same bends and straights.

10.2.2 TRACK DAY BENEFITS FOR ROAD RIDING

Despite the common misconception that track days are only suitable for racers or sports motorcycle enthusiasts, track days can help you to be safer, more prepared by increasing your control and reaction on public roads.

- **Enhanced Cornering Techniques:** Track riding focuses specifically on cornering, giving you experience in choosing the right lines and managing lean angles when travelling on the road. This skill will help you to enter corners more smoothly as a result of better handling on twisty roads.

- **Improved Braking and Acceleration Control:** Learning to brake at higher speeds and control throttle response in a controlled environment will help you react more effectively to potential hazards on the road. You can also get a better idea of how your motorcycle reacts to possible sudden emergency braking and learn how to manage it.

- **Reflexes and Situational Awareness:** Track days are fast paced and this will help you build faster reactions and reflexes, especially for hazard anticipation. This heightened awareness and ability to react will be useful on your motorcycle in heavy traffic on public roads, rural roads and unexpected road conditions.

10.2.3 INSURANCE CONSIDERATIONS FOR TRACK DAYS

Since participating in a track day is different from riding on public roads and involves more accident risk, there may be non-standard differences in insurance coverage. Therefore, checking what your insurance policy covers in terms of track days and acting accordingly will help you to take precautions in advance against problems that will arise later:

- **Standard Insurance Policies:** Generally, most motorcycle insurance policies exclude track days from coverage. This means that any damage to your motorcycle on the track, whether accidental or due to wear and tear, is usually not covered. Before attending a track day, it is a good idea to check your policy to see if track day coverage is included and consult your insurer if necessary.

- **Track Day Insurance:** There are some companies that specialise in track day insurance, to find these quickly you can contact the track you want to attend and ask for their recommendations. Track day insurance will usually cover damage to your motorcycle, but will not cover liability for injuries. The cost of these policies can vary depending on factors such as the model of your motorcycle, the venue and your level of experience.

- **Helmet and Leathers Coverage:** I mentioned that safety is at the forefront on track days, which means that the clothes you wear on the track should be good, but also costly. Some track day insurance may allow you to add additional coverage for protective gear, including helmets, gloves and leathers, which can be expensive to replace.

Tip: If you are considering taking out track day insurance, it is worth planning this in advance as some insurance providers may require additional documentation. Always read the policy details carefully, as insurance coverage can vary depending on the track location, speed limits and type of event.

10.3 BUILDING RIDER CONFIDENCE

Whether you are new to motorcycling or an experienced rider, you may struggle with self-confidence, especially if you've had a close call, an accident or have been away from riding for a while. As your confidence improves, you will be able to make better decisions and react quickly in challenging situations, which will improve your overall riding experience.

10.3.1 GRADUAL EXPOSURE TO DIFFERENT CONDITIONS

One of the best ways to build confidence is to gradually and consistently ride in different riding environments and conditions.

- **Start Small:** Start your rides by riding in familiar, low-traffic areas where you feel more in control. Then, as you begin to feel comfortable, gradually introduce more challenging routes such as heavier traffic, higher speeds or unfamiliar roads. After each successful ride, remind yourself what you did well.

- **Ride in All Weather Conditions:** The UK's unpredictable weather conditions such as rain, wind, fog and low temperatures will actually create the environment that will naturally prepare you for different conditions. Practising in light rain or light windy conditions will help you learn how to adjust braking and cornering techniques on your motorcycle.

- **Practice Essential Skills Regularly:** Regularly practising basic skills such as emergency braking, low speed control and cornering in an empty car park, with a focus on balance and handling, will help you develop muscle memory in these areas and prepare you for the unexpected on the road.

10.3.2 REBUILDING CONFIDENCE AFTER AN ACCIDENT

Although it is a situation that we do not want to happen to anyone, accidents are a part of life and can happen to anyone. A motorcycle rider who has been in an accident may experience fear and hesitation on the road. If you have had a fall or collision, you can follow these steps to get back to riding and regain your confidence on your motorcycle:

- **Controlled Environments:** Start by riding in car parks or quieter areas where you can practice riding your motorcycle at your own pace. You can gradually move towards roads with lighter traffic before moving on to more challenging routes. This will bring riding awareness that will gradually build your confidence.

- **Take a Refresher Course:** Professional refresher courses can help you identify and correct any riding habits you may have developed after your accident. Instructors will help you regain your self-confidence with their motivating feedback.

- **Ride with a Supportive Buddy:** If you are unable or unwilling to get professional support, you can instead ride with an experienced friend who can encourage you and share useful tips. Knowing that someone is behind you as you regain your skills will make you feel safer and more comfortable.

- **Set Realistic Goals:** Take your time and try to take small steps to regain your confidence. Start warming up by taking your rides on a specific route, in specific road conditions, and set achievable goals, such as mastering a specific skill.

- **Attend a "Biker Down" Course:** Biker Down training, delivered by the London Fire Brigade, seeks to equip motorcyclists with the knowledge and confidence to deal with these unwanted challenges for themselves and other motorcyclists, with advice on accident scene management, basic first aid specific to motorcyclists and advice on staying visible and safe whilst riding.

10.4 FILTERING AND OVERTAKING SAFELY

Filtering (or lane splitting) and overtaking, especially in urban riding, are practices that require attention and technique to perform safely on a motorcycle. When performed correctly, these manoeuvres will enrich your motorcycle riding experience and skills. However, it is important to have a good understanding of the rules and how you should apply them, as applying them inappropriately can lead to accidents or violations.

10.4.1 FILTERING THROUGH TRAFFIC

Unlike some countries, in the UK it is legal for motorcycles to filter or move appropriately between lanes of slow or stationary traffic, but they must be done with care to avoid accidents.

- **Understand the Legal Boundaries:** Filtering is a permitted practice in the UK, but when doing so, you must follow the rules of the road and only apply it in slow-moving or stationary traffic without causing disruption or danger to other drivers.

- **Safe Filtering Techniques:**

    - **Keep Speed Low:** When filtering in traffic with your motorcycle, try to keep your speed 10-15 miles above the flow of traffic in order to react to sudden movements.

    - **Stay Alert for Lane Changes:** Car drivers in particular are likely to make unexpected lane changes when traffic is stopped, often because they are not expecting someone to come from behind. Try to keep a safe distance from cars by constantly checking for signs such as turning wheels or turn signals.

    - **Avoid Filtering Near Junctions and Roundabouts:** Vehicles are more likely to change lanes around junctions, roundabouts and other passing areas, so proceed with caution or try to avoid filtering in these situations.

    - **Be Visible:** When travelling on the road on your motorcycle, try to position yourself where you can be seen in other drivers' mirrors so that they are aware of your presence and are less likely to cut in front of you unexpectedly or cause trouble.

10.4.2 OVERTAKING ON BUSY ROADS

Motorcycle overtaking requires skills that needs awareness and precision to execute properly, just like any other traffic vehicle. For your own and other drivers' safety, it is crucial to practise using the proper technique.

- **Understand the Rules for Overtaking:**
  - **Overtake on the Right:** Overtaking should always be done from the right in the UK, unless you are in slow traffic and the car on the right is stationary or moving more slowly than you are.
  - **Avoid Hazardous Locations:** Never overtake near pedestrian crossings, roundabouts, blind bends or hill ridges as there is a high risk of accidents and limited visibility.
- **Safe Overtaking Techniques:**
  - **Plan Your Overtake Carefully:** Before overtaking, make sure you have enough space and time to complete the manoeuvre safely. Determine the best time to move, check your mirrors, and lastly, always perform a shoulder check (**lifesaver look**) to make sure there are no other vehicles in your blind spots.
  - **Maintain a Safe Distance:** Try to leave enough space between you and the vehicles you overtake so that your mirrors or handlebars do not hit. In particular, other drivers may unexpectedly get in front of you or brake, increasing the risk of collision, in these

situations, the distance you establish will be useful by reducing your risk of accident.

    - **Return to Your Lane Smoothly:** After overtaking, make sure you are far enough away from the overtaken vehicle before returning to your lane and avoid sudden lane changes that may scare other drivers.

- **Practice Defensive Riding:** Both filtering and overtaking require a high level of awareness and control. Defensive techniques such as regularly checking mirrors, keeping your distance and using clear signals will help you anticipate the actions of other drivers, improving safety for you and all road users.

10.5 OFF-ROAD RIDING SKILLS

Learning off-road riding techniques is an excellent way to develop control, balance and general riding skills that can benefit you on normal roads in the same way that track days can. Unlike track days, off-road training teaches you how to manage your motorcycle in challenging conditions such as loose soil, mud and uneven surfaces. These adaptability and control skills will especially benefit you in bad weather conditions and on some of the UK's rough roads.

10.5.1 BENEFITS OF OFF-ROAD TRAINING

- **Enhanced Control:** Off-road riding requires you to manage the motorcycle's handling, suspension and stability on loose surfaces. Practising on gravel, mud and other unpredictable terrain helps you improve your throttle and brake control, which can mean more confidence on wet or bumpy roads.

- **Improved Reflexes:** As off-road terrain requires quick reactions to sudden changes such as rocks, potholes or unexpected turns, sharpening your reflexes will improve your ability to react quickly to road hazards, potholes or slippery surfaces.

- **Balance and Body Positioning:** Maintaining balance is one of the most necessary skills in off-road riding, you need to constantly adjust your body position to maintain balance. These adjustments will teach you better handling techniques and help you to keep your balance on road surfaces affected by rubble, oil leaks or ice patches that you may encounter in normal asphalt riding.

- **Confidence Building:** Facing and tackling challenging off-road conditions will give you a confidence boost, especially if you occasionally worry about normal road conditions or some bad weather conditions. Knowing that you can navigate more challenging terrain conditions will motivate you to succeed in riding on any kind of road.

10.5.2 POPULAR OFF-ROAD RIDING SCHOOLS IN THE UK

There are many reputable off-road riding schools in the UK, suitable for all skill levels from beginners to advanced off-road enthusiasts and offering training in a controlled environment with skilled instructors. Some of the popular schools include but are not limited to:

- **Yamaha Off-Road Experience (Wales):** This popular school in the Cambrian Mountains of Wales offers hands-on training sessions for all skill levels using Yamaha's WR, TT-R and Ténéré adventure motorcycles. Motorcycle riders learn basic skills such as throttle control in challenging conditions, braking on loose terrain and hill climbs useful for adventure riding.

- **BMW Off-Road Skills (Wales):** BMW's off-road course is ideal for adventure motorcycle enthusiasts, especially those interested in BMW GS models. From beginner to advanced, the course offers courses covering everything from balance and body positioning to advanced obstacle awareness. It is particularly suitable for motorcycle riders who want to improve their adventure travelling skills over rough terrain.

- **Dave Thorpe Honda Off-Road Centre (Devon):** Focusing on the basics of enduro riding, trail riding and motocross on Honda CRF dirt bikes, this course provides a powerful experience of braking, cornering and navigating challenging off-road trails.

- **Off The Kerb Adventure Rides:** Dorking-based Off The Kerb Adventure Rides offer a range of options from expertly guided one-day rides designed for both beginners and experienced riders, to two-day tours of areas such as Surrey and Dorset.

- **Ady Smith KTM Off-Road Experience (Various Locations):** Officially supported by KTM, this course offers sessions tailored to different skill levels with a focus on riding high performance off-road motorcycles. The course is based in Bristol, Matlock, North Wales and Stoke on Trent, covering basic techniques such as riding in sand, mud and gravel and managing rough and technical trails.

- **Triumph Adventure Experience (South Wales):** Ideal for Triumph riders and anyone interested in adventure-style riding, this course offers sessions on

Triumph motorcycle models. For those who want to improve their adventure touring skills, there is training in balance, traction control, braking on hills and riding on challenging tracks.

10.5.3 TIPS FOR GETTING THE MOST OUT OF OFF-ROAD TRAINING

- **Choose the Right Course for Your Skill Level:** If you are a beginner, opt for introductory courses to build a foundation before moving on to advanced terrain and techniques. Most schools offer tiered training sessions to suit different levels of experience, and you can find a course to suit your style that can develop you from beginner to advanced.

- **Wear Appropriate Gear:** Most off-road courses also offer the option to hire clothing. Since all the clothes you use for normal road use may not be suitable for off-road riding, you can consider the rental option of special equipment such as full-face helmets with goggles, body armour, gloves and boots designed for off-road use. Since off-road riding requires active body movements, if you make sure that your equipment is comfortable, protective and allows freedom of movement, you will have no problems on your rides.

- **Focus on Body Position:** Unlike road riding, off-road riding often requires standing on pegs to better control your motorcycle on uneven surfaces. You can practice setting your body position correctly, shifting your weight and standing to maintain balance and control.

- **Practice Throttle Control and Braking Techniques:** Off-road riding requires smooth throttle control and adaptive braking techniques. Since traction is low, especially on loose surfaces, learn to use the brakes "feather" (apply them lightly) and use the rear brake more, which is generally preferred for off-road riding.

- **Take It Slow:** Take your time on the course, remember that the aim is to acquire a solid skill and make it a habit to improve your riding control. Listen to what your instructor says, it is always information from experience and is valuable. Ask questions when necessary and spend time practising to learn each technique before moving on.

10.5.4 INSURANCE BENEFITS OF OFF-ROAD TRAINING

Although off-road training focuses on non-public roads, as the skills learnt can make you a safer, more confident rider on public roads, some insurers recognise the value of off-road training and may offer discounts to riders who complete accredited courses. So asking your insurance provider if any off-road courses could reduce your premiums could help you take advantage of getting a discount.

At the end, Off-road training will improve your control, overall riding experience and safety, so whether you're tackling a trail, commuting to work in challenging conditions or encountering unexpected situations on a daily ride, it will help you to deal with these situations with ease, adding to your confidence.

In this chapter, I've tried to explain that passing your motorcycle test is a great start, but you can continue to learn skills that will help you stay safer in a variety of riding conditions by attending advanced riding courses, track days and off-road riding.

11. MOTORCYCLE SECURITY: PROTECTING YOUR MOTORCYCLE FROM THEFT

Motorcycles are particularly vulnerable to theft due to their size and portability. This chapter covers essential security measures you can take to keep your motorcycle safe, from selecting high-quality locks and chains to installing advanced tracking systems. Whether you're parking at home or on the road, these tools and techniques can provide extra peace of mind.

11.1 UNDERSTANDING MOTORCYCLE THEFT RISKS

Motorcycle theft is a common problem in the UK, as it is in many countries, and motorcycles face higher theft rates than many other vehicles due to their unique vulnerabilities. Understanding the risks associated with theft is very important here, sometimes taking preventative measures, even very simple ones, can help you protect your motorcycle. Thieves often target high-value models that are left unattended for long periods of time in accessible areas or motorcycles with poor security. Between two motorcycles standing next to each other, thieves may gravitate towards the motorcycle with less security than the motorcycle with multiple layers of security.

I will try to summarise the most common theft tactics and countermeasures you can use to secure your motorcycle against these situations.

11.1.1 COMMON THEFT METHODS

- **Lift-and-Carry:** Smaller or lighter motorcycles, such as mopeds or scooters, are particularly vulnerable to lift-theft. Especially with these lighter types of motorcycles, thieves can physically lift the motorcycle and load it into a vehicle such as a van or lorry and drive away in seconds.
    - **Countermeasure:** Whenever possible, try to secure your motorcycle to an immovable object such as a ground anchor, post or designated motorcycle lock stand, especially if you have a motorcycle of this type that is small and light enough to be lifted by 2 or 3 people. If an anchor is not available, you can avoid the lift-and-go technique by locking your motorcycle to a nearby heavy object or another motorcycle.
- **Bolt-Cutting and Angle Grinders:** Many thieves use portable bolt cutters or angle grinders to break locks and chains. They can cut through with these devices, depending on the type of locks and chains you have installed. Although angle grinders are noisy, it is unfortunately true that these methods are often used during the day, even in crowded public places.
    - **Countermeasure:** Try to use high-quality, at least 14 mm thick, hardened steel chains and locks that are resistant to bolt cutters and require more time and noise to break with an angle grinder. When attaching your chain to your motorcycle,

position it high off the ground to make it more difficult to cut, especially with a bolt cutter. Although such chains and locks are heavy and not very practical to carry, they will provide a good advantage in terms of the safety of your motorcycle.

- **Roll-Away Theft:** If the wheels or frame are not secured in place to prevent your motorcycle from moving, thieves can easily push the motorcycle away by hand to a more secluded area to break the remaining security features.
    - **Countermeasure:** Many new motorcycles are equipped with handlebar locks, but don't rely on this to leave your motorcycle unattended. Because these handlebar locks can be easily broken by thieves with violence applied by hand or foot. Therefore, use disc locks or brake locks to immobilise the wheels, making it difficult for the thief to push the motorcycle away even if he breaks the handlebar lock. The combination of a disc lock and a heavy-duty chain lock will act as a deterrent to thieves.
- **Keyless Theft (Relay Theft):** This theft model, which is more common in cars, can also be applied to some motorcycles equipped with keyless ignition systems. With this method, thieves can use relay theft by using signal boosting devices to trick the motorcycle into thinking that the key is nearby.
    - **Countermeasure:** If you have a motorcycle with this type of keyless start feature, you can hide your key fob in a signal blocking pouch when the motorcycle is not in use. This can prevent thieves

from picking up the key signal and amplifying it with a relay to start your motorcycle.

- **Opportunistic Theft:** Sometimes, leaving your motorcycle unattended and unlocked, even for a few minutes, can be an invitation to opportunistic thieves.
    - **Countermeasure:** Always lock your motorcycle so that you don't regret it later, even if you are away for a short time. For additional protection, you can also use a motorcycle cover to reduce visibility and conceal high-value features.

11.1.2 HIGH-RISK LOCATIONS AND SITUATIONS

Having information about the condition and location of the place where you park your motorcycle and knowing what kind of precautions you can take will be one of the helpful factors that reduce the risk of theft.

- **Residential Areas with High Crime Rates:** Parking your motorcycle outside in areas with high theft rates can increase the risk. If possible in such areas, try to store your motorcycle in a locked garage, if you do not have such a possibility, increase the security of your motorcycle by securing it with multiple locks and anchors.

- **Public Parking Lots:** Although theft is also possible where there are CCTV cameras or security personnel, car parks without these are commonly preferred by thieves. Try to choose locations with anchor points or designated motorcycle bays monitored by security cameras.

- **Event or Festival Parking:** Crowded gatherings and areas that often lack fixed security measures because they are temporary, mean crowded parking areas that can attract thieves. You can plan to attend events with secure parking options, even if only temporarily, or park your motorcycle within sight of security personnel.

- **Long-Term Parking:** Try to use multiple security devices, including GPS trackers, to protect your motorcycle during long-term parking, as leaving your motorcycle in one place for long periods of time, such as an airport or hotel, can make it more vulnerable to planned theft. If you are staying in a hotel, inform the hotel staff about your motorcycle before you make your hotel reservation and clarify whether they have a parking space in a visible, secure area.

11.1.3 TIME OF DAY AND SECURITY AWARENESS

Motorcycle theft can happen at any time of the day, but statistically it is most likely to happen in the evening and at night when visibility is low and there are fewer people around. Especially at such times, taking a few extra precautions will be useful to ensure the safety of your motorcycle.

- **Night Security Measures:** At night, try to park in well-lit areas with heavy pedestrian traffic. Deserted places with few people passing by will harbour a high risk of theft. If you park at home, placing lights with motion sensors around your garage or driveway can deter potential thieves.

- **Daytime Security Awareness:** As I mentioned at the beginning, although more risky at night, daytime theft are also very common. Thieves can disguise themselves as motorcycle transport or service workers to attract less attention. Even if you leave your motorcycle for a short time during the day, make sure that it is either in your field of vision or secured with sufficient locks and chains.

11.1.4 SEASONAL THEFT TRENDS

Motorcycle theft increases during peak riding seasons (spring and summer) as motorcycles are used more often and left in public places.

- **Peak Season Caution:** During the riding season, avoid leaving your motorcycle in unfamiliar or heavily trafficked areas for long periods of time. To help you decide where to park, you can check local motorcycle forums or police reports for areas where thefts have increased recently. Although this is not something you can do every time, it will be in your best interest to be sensitive to this issue, as situations where you need to leave it for long periods of time are usually a pre-planned activity.

- **Winter Storage:** When the season is over, if you don't use your motorcycle very often, you may want to consider investing in a storage solution such as a locked shed or a garage with anchor to prevent theft.

11.1.5 THE VALUE OF A LAYERED SECURITY APPROACH

The most important approach to motorcycle security is to apply layered security measures. Combining more than one security measure, such as an anchor, a heavy-duty chain, a disc lock with alarm and a motorcycle cover, will increase the time, effort and risk a thief will encounter, so you can provide a level of protection that few thieves will attempt.

- **Tip:** If you have relocated to a new location or purchased a new motorcycle, it is extremely helpful to periodically review your security setup. Upgrading security measures where possible and adapting to new risks will help to ensure the safety of your motorcycle.

11.2 ESSENTIAL SECURITY TOOLS

Thieves often target motorcycles with minimal protection, so a layered approach combining physical deterrents and advanced technology to secure your motorcycle will increase the security of your motorcycle. Below I have tried to share the basic tools and techniques to consider.

11.2.1 LOCKS AND CHAINS

Locks and chains are security equipment that are critical in creating a physical deterrent to theft, especially when combined with a fixed object or anchor.

- **Chains:** Try to invest in chains made of hardened steel with a minimum thickness of 14mm, which provide significant resistance to portable bolt cutters. If you park your motorcycle outdoors, try to choose chains with an anti-corrosion coating to ensure a long chain life.
    - **Tip:** The thicker the chain, the greater the deterrent. If the chain is long enough to allow you to wrap it around both the frame of your motorcycle and an anchor point without leaving slack, it will make it difficult to cut with bolt cutters.
- **Locks:** Try to invest in locks with approved high security ratings such as **Sold Secure** or **Thatcham**. U-

locks and disc locks made of hardened steel or with double locking mechanisms are security locks that make it very difficult (but not impossible) for thieves to manipulate.

- **Positioning:** Try to position the lock high off the ground to make it difficult for thieves to apply leverage with bolt cutters. If the chain is long enough, try to secure it to the frame or swing-arm of the motorcycle rather than the wheel alone.

11.2.2 GROUND ANCHORS

A ground anchor is a permanent piece of security equipment and method that provides a secure point in your home or garage that cannot be moved to lock your motorcycle. Anchoring your motorcycle to a fixed object adds an additional layer of security, especially against the theft of your motorcycle by roll-away theft.

- **Installation:** While most ground anchors will require installation in concrete or brick surfaces, ground anchors are also available that can be installed by digging into the ground and embedded in concrete. If you are going to make this type of installation in your home, try to install it in an area out of direct line of sight to reduce visibility to passersby.

- **Types of Anchors**

    - **Bolt-Down Anchors:** These anchors bolt directly to existing concrete surfaces such as driveways or garage floors, providing a permanent and solid fixed security point for your motorcycle. This model anchors are ideal for outdoor or garage use.

- **Wall-Mounted Anchors:** They are designed for smaller spaces such as narrow garages or for fixing to walls where the floor is not concrete. By securing your motorcycle higher off the ground with a chain, they make it more difficult for thieves to manipulate the lock or chain with support from the ground.

- **Portable Anchors:** Lightweight and easy to install, portable anchors are a temporary practical solution for campers and travellers. While not as robust as fixed options, they provide an additional layer of security in travelling situations where you need to park away from home.

- **Dig-In Anchors:** Dig-In anchors are buried in the ground and fixed with cement to form a completely immobile fixture, providing the ultimate in security. They are a little more labour intensive to install than others, but in return you get the ultimate in security. Firstly a hole is dug, the anchor is inserted and the surrounding area is filled with cement to secure it in place. These anchors are perfect for long term installations and as the anchor is fixed into the ground with concrete, the only thing thieves can do is force the chain.

- **Tip:** Use a heavy-duty chain with your anchor and plan to position the motorcycle and anchor in a way that makes it difficult for thieves to access the chain without moving the motorcycle, and you will maximise security.

11.2.3 DISC LOCKS AND WHEEL LOCKS

Portable locks are one of the handy portable options for immobilising your motorcycle, especially in short-term parking situations.

- **Disc Locks:** If your motorcycle has disc brakes, compact and easy-to-carry disc locks secure to the brake disc and prevent the wheel from spinning, making it harder for thieves to roll the bike. Some models also come with a built-in alarm that emits a loud sound when the disc lock is tampered with, providing an important deterrent.
    - **Tip:** Always use a brightly coloured reminder cable in the shape of a spring that connects to your handlebars. This will help prevent the common mistake of forgetting that you have installed a disc lock while the lock is still engaged and setting off, which can damage your disc and brake system.
- **U-Locks:** U-locks are versatile, heavy-duty locks that can secure your motorcycle's wheel or frame to a fixed object such as a ground anchor or sturdy post, or if wide enough, you can attach them directly to your wheel. These locks are designed to be larger and usually heavier than disc locks to resist cutting tools and leverage attacks.
    - **Tip:** Position the lock high off the ground to make it difficult to use cutting tools effectively.
- **Brake Lever Locks:** Brake lever locks are compact devices that clamp onto your brake lever and engage the brake system, immobilising your motorcycle by continuous braking. They are easy to install and

remove, less secure than disc locks and U-locks, but practical and useful for very short stops.

  - **Tip:** For added security, especially in high-risk areas, combine the brake lever lock with another locking method such as a disc lock, U-lock or chain when parking to further increase the security of your motorcycle.

11.2.4 ALARMS AND IMMOBILISERS

Alarms and immobilisers are electronic deterrents, making it difficult to start the motorcycle without the correct key or raising awareness by triggering a loud alarm when tampering is detected.

- **Alarms:** Motorcycle alarm systems are useful in that when they detect movement or tampering, they emit a loud sound to alert bystanders, or notify you depending on the type of alarm, that something is wrong.
  - **Tip:** Some alarm systems will notify you even if you are not with your motorcycle, so investing in an alarm system that has the ability to notify you remotely if it has been tampered with will help you to be aware of problems even when you are not always with your motorcycle.
- **Immobilisers:** Usually come integrated with alarm systems, providing an additional layer of protection by preventing your engine from starting without the correct key or key fob.
  - **Tip:** An immobiliser with a kill-switch option will act as a secondary deterrent by being

hidden on your motorcycle, preventing thieves from hot-wiring or starting the engine.

11.2.5 GPS TRACKERS AND RECOVERY DEVICES

GPS trackers and recovery devices allow you to track the location of your motorcycle in real time and are the most effective modern security devices that can help in recovery if your motorcycle is stolen.

- **Installation:** There are many small GPS trackers designed for motorcycles, and it is usually recommended to install them in a hidden place on the motorcycle so that they are not easy to find. Usually the professional brands recommend that they are installed by professionals to ensure that they are installed in the most hidden place possible.

- **Features to Look For:**

    - **Real-Time Tracking:** Trackers with real time GPS will allow you to track the location of your motorcycle from your phone.

    - **RF Tracking:** In the event of theft, devices and services with Radio Frequency tracking, can physically go to the last GPS location and accurately locate the motorcycle up to 1 metre.

    - **Geo-Fencing:** Some GPS units will allow you to put a boundary around your motorcycle and you will receive an alert if your motorcycle goes outside of that area.

    - **Battery Life:** Long battery life is important with this type of device, and units that are connected to the motorcycle's battery for continuous charging are important to keep working for a long time even if the motorcycle's battery is disconnected.

- **Subscription Costs:** Many monitoring services require a subscription for real-time monitoring and alerts. Some services have call centres where real people call you to ask if there is a problem when the devices detect a problem. This type of service costs more than others, but can be reassuring, so it's worth comparing monthly costs to make sure it fits your budget.

11.2.6 MOTORCYCLE COVERS AND ADDITIONAL TIPS

While not a primary security measure, and sometimes not even considered a security measure, a motorcycle cover reduces visibility and is an additional layer of security that can prevent opportunistic theft by concealing the make and model of the motorcycle.

- **Cover Benefits:** Covers help prevent incentivised theft by concealing your motorcycle's make and high-value modifications. Thieves are less likely to target a motorcycle they can't identify or don't know what security measures are under the cover.
- **Weather-Resistant Covers:** Especially if you park outdoors, try to opt for a waterproof, weatherproof cover so you can keep your motorcycle dry and protected from weather damage.
- **Tip:** Try to choose a cover with lockable rings so that you can secure it with a chain or lock, helping to keep the cover in place and adding a small but useful additional barrier against theft.

11.3 PRACTICAL TIPS FOR EVERYDAY SECURITY

Everyday safety habits will be just as important as investing in physical and electronic security devices.

11.3.1 PARKING TECHNIQUES

- **Choose Safe Locations:** To deter thieves, try to park in well-lit, crowded areas rather than in isolated locations whenever possible.
- **Angle Parking:** If possible, park your motorcycle at an angle that makes it difficult to lift and carry, or position it in a way that makes it difficult to move and hold.
- **Covering:** A motorcycle cover, especially one that does not show a brand name, will make your motorcycle less noticeable and harder to identify, making it less likely to attract potential thieves.

11.3.2 LAYERED SECURITY

Creating a layered defence system by using multiple types of security together is perhaps the biggest secret of security habits.

- **Combine Tools:** Try to increase the number of layers by using a disk lock, ground anchor and a chain at the same time, especially if you are going to park for a long time.
- **Rotate Parking Spots:** To make your motorcycle less predictable, especially in commuting situations, try to park it in different places on a rotating basis rather than in the same spot every day to make it less

predictable, which can protect you from planned thief attacks.

- **Tip:** If you have luggage system, keep a portable lock and a disk lock, or a U-lock that you can attach to the frame to secure your motorcycle wherever you go. Disc locks are also quite small, so you can easily carry them under the saddle or in a backpack (use back protector if you use backpack for carrying lock).

11.3.3 MAINTAINING YOUR SECURITY DEVICES

Check your safety devices regularly to ensure they remain effective.

- **Check for Wear:** Inspect chains, locks and anchors for wear and tear, as well as for rust or weaknesses that could compromise their safety, and try to replace them when you think they are weak.

- **Recharge Trackers:** If your tracker is predominantly powered by the motorcycle's battery and you are not riding, especially on a daily basis, try to check the charge regularly.

- **Alarms and Batteries:** Regularly test alarms and immobilisers before and after every ride to make sure they are always ready and replace the batteries if necessary.

11.4 SECURITY FOR LONG-DISTANCE AND OVERNIGHT PARKING

When you go on tour with your motorcycle or stay overnight in unfamiliar places, it will be important to plan in advance to park your motorcycle in a way that prioritises the safety of your motorcycle in the places you go to reduce the risk of theft of your motorcycle.

Hotels and Overnight Stops

When staying on the road, try to choose hotels or accommodations with well-lit parking lots.

- **Secure Parking:** Some hotels may provide secure or gated parking with CCTV surveillance, and some accommodations, especially those with motorcyclist-friendly services, may even provide dedicated motorcycle parking with locked ground anchors or gated sections.
    - **Tip:** When booking, it can be very important to contact ahead and inquire about motorcycle-friendly features such as secure parking or gated areas, some hotels even offer special parking arrangements for motorcyclists, so don't hesitate to ask. If a hotel is not safe enough for you, it may be worth looking at other hotels.
- **Indoor or Covered Parking:** Accommodations that offer indoor or covered parking will provide an advantage in protecting your motorcycle from theft and will also help protect your motorcycle from the weather on long journeys.
    - **Tip:** Smaller guesthouses or hostels, especially if they do not have dedicated motorcycle parking, may allow you to park closer to the property if you discuss it in advance, thus reducing the risk of theft as your motorcycle will be more visible.

Use Multiple Locks

A combination of several security devices will significantly increase the time and effort required to steal your motorcycle, making it less attractive to thieves.

- **Chain and Disc Lock Combo:** If possible, try to secure your motorcycle with a sturdy chain attached to a solid object (such as a pole or anchor). At the same time, you can take additional precautions by preventing the wheels from turning with a disk lock.
    - **Tip:** When using chains, you can provide extra security by passing your motorcycle through the frame or swing-arm if possible, not just the wheel.
- **Tracker and Alarm:** If your motorcycle has a GPS tracker, activate it during the night. You can also set all immobilisers or alarms to high sensitivity to ensure that you will be notified in the slightest situation.
- **Cover Your Bike:** A simple cover can easily prevent ordinary theft by hiding the make and model of your motorcycle from prying eyes.
    - **Tip:** Using a durable cover with locking holes to secure it to your motorcycle is a small but effective way to prevent tampering.

Research Safe Parking Options

Be sure to do your research in advance to find safe overnight parking spaces, especially in busy areas or cities.

- **Local Forums and Motorcycling Apps:** Search online communities, forums or apps in your destination area for other motorcyclists' suggestions for safe motorcycle-friendly parking.

- **Communicate with Other Riders:** If you are touring in a group, decide on your parking options in advance and try to park your motorcycles together. Tying your motorcycles together when parking together will also help as an extra layer of security against theft.

Final Tips for Long-Distance Security

- **Set a Routine:** Try to get into the habit of securing your motorcycle every night in a specific order, making sure to apply all layers of safety.

- **Plan Ahead:** Especially if you are passing through or staying in high-risk areas, make sure to research and plan in advance where you can park along your route.

- **Secure Your Gear:** If you have bags or a storage bag, remember to lock them or take valuables with you overnight. Thieves are often opportunistic and visible equipment will be an easy target for them.

11.5 INSURANCE CONSIDERATIONS

Approved safety equipment and devices that you use to effectively secure your motorcycle can reduce your insurance premiums as many insurers offer discounts.

11.5.1 SECURITY DEVICES AND PREMIUMS

- **Approved Locks and Alarms:** The list of approved locks, alarms and trackers may vary from insurer to insurer, so investing in the right equipment in consultation with your insurer will help you get potential discounts.

- **Garage Storage Discounts:** Many insurance companies offer significant discounts for storing your motorcycle in a secure garage, but not all garages may accepted for discounts. For this, it will be useful to contact your insurer and ask which conditions you will get a discount with a garage that meets the conditions.

- **Tip:** Insurers apply discounts based on your declaration, but in the event of a theft, your insurer may ask you for some evidence. It is therefore a good idea to take receipts or photographs of the security equipment you have declared in the insurance.

11.5.2 GAP INSURANCE FOR HIGH-VALUE MOTORCYCLES

- **Consider Gap Insurance:** Gap insurance is an important and often overlooked type of insurance that you should consider taking out if you have a high-value or financed motorcycle. In the event of a total loss, gap insurance can cover the difference between the current market value of your motorcycle and the value you owe, saving you from a serious loss.

- **Review Coverage:** Not all insurance policies will cover the full cost of a stolen motorcycle, you should make sure you have adequate coverage based on the value of your motorcycle and security measures.

In this chapter, I have tried to focus on how you should take precautions against the threats of motorcycle theft that none of us want to experience, but are real. By applying these layers of protection, you will reduce your theft risks and have more peace of mind.

12. TOURING AND LONG-DISTANCE RIDING ON MOTORCYCLES

Touring and long-distance riding is a fun activity and very popular among motorcyclists, where you may want to escape from daily routines, go on an adventure to different places, test your motorcycle's capabilities. However, without careful preparation to ensure both comfort and safety on long-distance journeys, the whole ride can turn into a grind. In this chapter, I will try to share what you need and need to know for a successful tour, from choosing luggage systems to planning scenic routes.

12.1 TOURING ESSENTIALS

A successful and trouble-free motorcycle tour starts with good preparation. Both you and your motorcycle should be fully prepared for the journey. Here I will try to share about the essential motorcycle preparation you need to do before starting a long distance ride.

12.1.1 LUGGAGE SYSTEMS

It is very important to get a luggage system suitable for your motorcycle, riding style and personal preferences in order to carry your belongings in a safe and protected way, to have a smooth ride and to continue riding without stopping.

- **Hard Panniers and Top Cases:** Produced by many popular brands such as **GIVI**, **SW-Motech** and **Shad**, hard bags, which are ideal for long tours, offer high security due to their weather-resistant and lockable nature. Hard bags are recommended models because they provide extra protection for your belongings, especially in unpredictable weather conditions.

- **Soft Luggage:** Soft luggage options from brands such as Kriega and Oxford offer greater flexibility and are often preferred for different applications due to their lighter weight than hard bags. Similar to hard bags, soft luggage is also weatherproof, but you may need to make sure it has a waterproof lining as not all of them may be waterproof. These types of bags are preferred for those who have a sports motorcycle, or for riders who plan to travel off-road, as they do not break like hard bags when dropped, and are easy to remove and carry with you.

- **Tank Bags and Tail Bags:** Tank bags are relatively small bags that can be placed on top of your motorcycle tank for quick access to essentials such as your phone, wallet maps and water bottle. Tail bags are compact bags suitable for storing your tools, extra clothes or snacks. If you are going to use them in rainy weather, it would be useful to choose the ones with waterproof features. Both options are versatile solutions for riders on shorter tours, rider who doesn't want bulky luggage system and for motorcycles that cannot be fitted with fixed luggage attachments.

12.1.2 NAVIGATION AND TOOLS

On a long tour, especially if you are exploring unfamiliar areas, reliable navigation and essential tools are vital necessities during your journey.

- **GPS Systems:** Motorcycle-specific GPS units such as the **TomTom Rider** and **Garmin Zumo** are built for the harsh conditions motorcycles face, with features such as waterproofing and vibration resistance. Many models can include customisable scenic routes and weather updates to help you plan a smoother journey, so if you need these features, it's worth looking into the devices in detail before investing.

- **Smartphone Apps:** Apps such as **Calimoto**, **Scenic**, **Waze** and **Google Maps** are popular smartphone apps among UK riders. Motorcycle-specific apps such as Calimoto and Scenic will help you navigate more enjoyable routes by avoiding motorways and focusing on winding, scenic routes.

- **CarPlay and Android Auto Devices:** CarPlay or Android Auto, which also comes as a separate screen on some motorcycles, are recently popularised devices that you can buy separately and use applications on your phones with the physical structure of GPS systems. Smartphone applications compatible with these devices communicate wirelessly to these external displays and help you use your favourite motorcycle navigation applications without taking out your smartphone.

- **Toolkit:** A compact toolkit is essential to handle minor repairs. There are multi-purpose tools that can help with chain adjustments, tyre repairs and other minor maintenance tasks. Don't forget to carry repair kits, especially puncture repair kit for the tyres that are most likely to cause problems, and spare fuses with values appropriate to your motorcycle.

12.2 PLANNING ROUTES

Whether you are staying in the UK or travelling abroad, you can minimise unexpected difficulties and make your tour more enjoyable by careful route planning.

12.2.1 SETTING GOALS FOR YOUR RIDE

Before diving into mapping and directions, try to consider the main objectives of your tour. Each rider may have different priorities, especially if you are touring in a group, so try to discuss these and come up with a common goal, which will help you shape the best route:

- **Scenic Views:** If touring on scenic roads is a priority, you can work on routes that will allow you to travel along mountain roads, coastlines such as sea and lake, or rural areas.

- **Historical Sites:** If you are more interested in culture and history, you can research historical milestones or famous places online in advance and combine them with beautiful roads.

- **Technical Riding:** If you want to challenge yourself and your riding skills, routes with winding roads, elevation changes or mountain passes are exactly the places you should include in your route for these purposes.

- **Relaxation and Leisure:** Whatever the goal of a motorcycle tour, it requires long hours of travelling on a motorcycle. If you want to travel at a relaxed pace, you may want to choose routes with plenty of rest stops, scenic roads and comfortable accommodation.

Tip: Be realistic about the amount of time you have, try to plan for about twice the amount of time that your sat nav software gives you for the ride, especially as there will be stops, refuelling, etc. If you only have a few days, try to plan a shorter route with plenty of stops and sightseeing rather than taking the risk of trying to cover too many miles.

12.2.2 RESEARCHING THE ROUTE

After you have set your goals, you can now start the next part, the route research and planning phase, where you will go into more detail and spend more time. Here I will try to mention some methods to make your planning effective:

- **Use Navigation Apps and Websites:** Apps like **MyRoute-app** and **Calimoto** are practical apps for motorcyclists that help you find scenic routes or roads with less traffic. These apps can provide routes that you can build completely from scratch, as well as ready-made routes prepared by other motorcycle riders, often winding, scenic routes. You can change this kind of route about the region you will go to according to your wishes and create a route suitable for your destination.

- **Check Motorcycle Forums, Social Media and Motorcycle Magazines:** Rider forums, social media groups and some motorcycle magazines occasionally offer route suggestions and travel advice for specific areas. Experienced riders often share route maps, riding tips and points of interest, and you can use these maps directly or edit them to make them more suitable for the route you want.

- **Use Physical Maps:** Sometimes a detailed physical map can be very useful, with regional maps identifying scenic routes with symbols of hidden beauties that you cannot find on digital maps or that you cannot easily see. You may also find it useful to consult Michelin maps, which have set a standard for exploring scenic routes and are available in digital and print versions.

- **Government and Tourism Websites:** Many local tourism organisations publish recommended scenic routes that are ideal for motorcyclists. In the UK, websites for national parks or scenic byways may offer suggestions, including popular routes such as the North Coast 500 (NC500) or Atlantic Highway.

Tip: You'll be travelling through areas of the UK with limited cellular service, especially if you're planning an out-of-town tour by motorcycle. So print out a backup of your route or download it to your device if your navigation app has offline capability.

12.2.3 ROUTE PLANNING FOR FUEL AND STOPS

On long-distance journeys, careful planning for fuel stops, rest stops and meals will increase your comfort and reduce fatigue at the same time.

- **Identify Fuel Stations in Remote Areas:** In rural or mountainous areas, fuel stations will be scarce, so it is useful to do fuel planning well. Especially when planning the route, it is important to try to determine the fuel points in advance so that your journey is not interrupted. The **PetrolPrices** application in the UK can help you plan economically by showing the current prices of fuel stations.

- **Plan Scenic Stops:** You can divide the journey into parts by designating scenic viewpoints and landmarks as stopovers. Such breaks will make the journey more enjoyable and give you a chance to rest and recharge yourself.

- **Rest and Meal Breaks:** Regular breaks every 1-2 hours are important to prevent fatigue. In addition to refuelling stations, you can add roadside cafes, small towns or national park areas that provide a pleasant atmosphere for relaxing and eating to your route for these purposes.

Tip: If you are travelling through high altitude or remote areas, fuel stops will be even more critical. To avoid unexpectedly running low on fuel or being stranded without fuel, refuel at every available station in these areas. There are usually very few refuelling stations in such areas, so try to choose locations with other refuelling stations nearby just in case, as sometimes the maps may not have been updated and the refuelling station may no longer be in operation.

12.3 INTERNATIONAL TRAVEL: DOCUMENTS AND INSURANCE

If you intend to take your tour outside the UK and are planning to cross to other countries within Europe, there are additional legal requirements that need to be considered.

12.3.1 INSURANCE AND BREAKDOWN COVER

- **Insurance:** Before travelling abroad, you need to make sure that your UK motorcycle insurance covers international travel. Some insurers, such as **Bennetts** and **Devitt**, offer packages that include European cover, but if you already have insurance, it's a good idea to check with your insurer to make sure that the countries you're travelling to are covered so that you don't have a headache later on if something unexpected happens. If your insurance does not cover this, you can take out separate insurance for a certain period of time to cover international motorcycle travel.

- **Breakdown Cover:** For peace of mind outside of insurance, international breakdown cover can be very useful in case your motorcycle breaks down. Providers such as **Green Flag**, **AA** and **RAC** offer European breakdown options that include roadside assistance and towing if required, so if you already have cover from these companies, it's worth checking that it covers the European countries you'll be travelling to. These packages can be very useful options to avoid high costs abroad should mechanical problems arise.

12.3.2 DOCUMENTS TO CARRY

I will try to compile below a list of recommended documents to have with you for international riding:

- **Passport:** It is required for entry to most countries, especially after Brexit, and make sure that it is valid for at least 6 months covering your planned return. Although not all countries question this 6-month issue, it will be useful to pay attention to this in order to avoid problems in some countries.

- **UK Driving Licence:** You are not legally required to carry your driving licence on you at all times in the

UK, but don't forget to take your licence with you as every country has different laws abroad.

- **Insurance Documents:** Keep proof of both your UK and international cover with you, physically or digitally if possible. In some cases, if you are stopped by local enforcement on the road and cannot access online, physical documents will be useful here.

- **Motorcycle V5C Logbook:** Your motorcycle's registration certificate is essential to verify ownership of your motorcycle. You need to carry it with you abroad, especially after Brexit.

- **International Driving Permit (IDP):** Most EU countries accept UK driving licences, but you may be asked for an IDP when you cross into some other countries in Europe. Whichever countries you are travelling to, make sure you check in advance if this is a requirement.

12.4 RIDING COMFORT: STAYING COMFORTABLE ON LONG RIDES

On long journeys, it is important to prevent fatigue and to continue riding comfortably in order to reduce risks. For this purpose, maintaining your comfort by paying attention to your posture, fluid intake and rest stops is essential for efficient riding.

12.4.1 POSTURE AND ERGONOMICS

- **Seating Position:** A comfortable seat is very important to reduce fatigue as you will stay on your seat for very long periods of time on long journeys. For many motorcycle models, brands such as Sargent and Corbin produce alternative seats. If you don't think your seat is very comfortable, you may want to consider investing in special seats designed for touring, which can make a big difference on long journeys.

- **Handlebar Adjustments:** Adjusting your handlebars to a comfortable position will relieve pressure on your wrists and shoulders, preventing strain. You can make it comfortable for yourself by adding a riser to the handlebar. In addition, if your motorcycle has cruise control, these will also help reduce wrist fatigue on long journeys.

- **Foot Pegs:** If you are riding a sport or adventure bike, adjustable foot pegs that offer a more comfortable angle will also be a great additional comfort element to customise your riding position.

12.4.2 HYDRATION AND REST STOPS

- **Hydration:** When riding a motorcycle, you may become dehydrated without realising it, which can indirectly lead to fatigue and reduced concentration, so it is useful to take regular water breaks. If you can't think of drinking water while riding, a CamelBak water bag or similar device will help you quench your thirst without the need for frequent breaks.

- **Regular Breaks:** Try to take breaks every 90 minutes or so to stretch and refresh, taking into account weather conditions and other factors. This will help prevent stiffness that occurs during prolonged riding and increase your focus on the road.

12.5 HOW TO PACK FOR A MOTORCYCLE TOUR

Packing for a motorcycle tour requires a careful balance between identifying essential items, maintaining the balance of the motorcycle and keeping the luggage light. Whether you are going on a short weekend trip or a multi-day international journey, packing strategically can make a significant difference to comfort and safety. In this section, I will try to bring together basic, useful and efficient packing tips, taking into account different trip lengths.

12.5.1 PACKING ESSENTIALS: THE MUST-HAVES

These are the essentials that you must take with you on every motorcycle tour, whether short or long.

- **Protective Gear:** Helmets, gloves, jackets, trousers and boots with appropriate protection should be with you on every short or long trip. Considering modular helmets and gear with ventilated or removable lining for more comfort and comfort will help you adapt to different temperature conditions.

- **Motorcycle Toolkit:** Especially on long journeys or tours in remote areas, you may experience unexpected mechanical problems in an unexpected place. For this, having tyre repair kits, chain oil, adjustable wrenches, screwdrivers and a multi-purpose tool in a basic tool kit will be very useful when you are in such a situation.

- **First Aid Kit:** A first aid kit with basic supplies such as adhesive bandages, antiseptic wipes, painkillers, tweezers and gauze can be very useful. If you have an allergic condition, antihistamines and prescription medicines for problems you may experience due to flies or climate on the tour, be sure to add them to this bag.

- **Navigation Tools:** Since the possibilities brought by technology in recent times have made it very easy for us to navigate, a special motorcycle GPS for navigation, a phone holder where you can plug in your smartphone and offline map-enabled applications are now a must-have.

- **Identification and Documentation:** If you are travelling internationally, always carry a copy of your driving licence, insurance documents, V5C register and passport. In addition, for security, keeping digital backups on your phone will be useful in case of theft.

Packing Tip: Try to put your essential items that you may need often, such as your phone, wallet, etc., in an easily accessible place so that you can quickly retrieve them without unpacking your entire belongings.

12.5.2 BETTER-TO-HAVE ITEMS: ADDITIONAL COMFORTS AND CONVENIENCE

Although some products do not necessarily need to be with you, they are things that can optionally increase your comfort and convenience on long tours.

- **Waterproof Gear:** If your equipment is not waterproof, always pack waterproof outer layers for sudden downpours, even if the weather forecast is clear. Waterproof jackets, gloves and boot covers will also come in handy in extreme downpours.

- **Hydration Pack:** Especially in hot climates or long distances, you can use a water bag to meet your water needs without stopping.

- **Portable Power Bank:** Since you will have at least your phone with you on a motorcycle trip, it is important to keep them charged for safety and convenience. A small, high-capacity power bank is a must-have if you are using multiple devices or camping.

- **Extra Layers and Base Layers:** As touring is a long-term activity, temperatures can vary significantly during this period, so additional layers and thermal base-layers layers will help you be prepared for both cold mornings and hot afternoons.

- **Earplugs:** Although this is an issue that many motorcycle riders overlook, especially on tours, you will be exposed to engine and wind noise for long hours, so it is important to use quality earplugs that reduce stress and protect hearing to prevent fatigue caused by this.

- **Dry Bags:** Dry bags are important to protect clothes, electronic devices and documents from rain, splashes and moisture. Even if you have a hard case, you can provide extra protection by using a dry bag inside.

Packing Tip: Since load weight and balance are important on a motorcycle, try to prioritise lightweight, compact versions for comfortable items.

12.5.3 SUGGESTED PACKING LISTS BY TRIP DURATION

Depending on the length of your tour and how far you are travelling, the things you need to take to effectively meet your needs will vary, here I will try to share some suggestions for different trip lengths:

Day Trips or Overnight
For short trips, try to focus on the essentials and minimise your load.

- **Basic Essentials:** Helmet, protective clothing, navigation tools and first aid kit are the most basic needs that should be with you at a minimum on all your rides.

- **Small Toolkit:** You can create a tool kit with puncture repair material and a multi-purpose tool that can solve minor problems.

- **Water and Snacks:** For one-day or overnight trips, it will be enough to take liquid and a few light snacks with you.

- **Portable Charger:** A small power bank will be enough to keep your devices working.

  Packing Tip: You can use a tank bag or a compact rear bag for day trips to keep your motorcycle light and stable.

Weekend to 3-Day Trips
For trips of up to three days, you will need to take into account weather changes, basic personal items and comfort in addition to the items you would take on a day trip.

- **Extra Clothing:** You can take one or two spare clothes that are moisture wicking and quick drying.

- **Rain Gear and Extra Layers:** Since there may be unexpected rain or temperature drops even on day trips in the UK, you can definitely add layers such as raincoats and extra underwear that you can keep up with temperature changes on tours of this length.

- **Portable Toiletries:** You can bring a small towel, toothbrush and other basic toiletries in compact travel sizes as you will be staying on a trip of this length.

- **Food Storage and Light Cooking Gear:** If you plan on camping, a small, portable stove and a few dry or canned foods will come in handy.

  Packing Tip: If you use panniers or saddle bags for side storage, you can use one bag for clothes and toiletries and another for food, tools and emergency supplies.

Multi-Day and International Tours
You can prepare for long tours by considering the needs for self-sufficiency and products that help with additional comfort.

- **Clothing Layers and Extra Pairs:** Try to consider technical or merino wool base layers that are lightweight and moisture-wicking, especially if you are touring in multiple climates. Such products will help you move comfortably by helping to balance body temperature against the climate changes you will go to.

- **Repair Supplies:** Along with a slightly more comprehensive toolkit, you can add extra materials such as chain oil, fuses, spare bulbs and duct tape for quick repairs, enabling you to produce solutions on your own in many conditions.

- **Camping Gear:** If you are planning to camp, you need to pay particular attention to weight. In particular, you should try to choose camping equipment such as tents, sleeping bags and compact cooking equipment as light as possible. Choosing specially designed equipment that does not take up space, such as a compact stove, nesting cooking pots and a portable camping chair, will help you create a more balanced load.

- **International Documentation:** For international tours, carry additional documents such as an International Driving Permit, visa (if required) and contact details for embassies and local emergency services both in physical paper form and digitally on your phone.

  Packing Tip: Using a combination of hard bags for durability and safety will be useful for such long tours. On the other hand, combining with waterproof dry bags will make an extra contribution to keeping your belongings dry. Using a top bag for items that you will access frequently, such as snacks, tool bags, etc., will make your job easier in such urgent and short jobs.

12.5.4 PACKING FOR BALANCE AND WEIGHT DISTRIBUTION

Balancing your luggage weight on a motorcycle is very important to ensure safe use and rider comfort.

- **Distribute Weight Evenly:** Heavier items should be low and close to the motorcycle's centre of gravity, preferably in saddlebags or panniers, not on top. Otherwise, the motorcycle will be in a top-heavy position and will be difficult to control.

- **Secure Your Luggage:** Make sure that all bags are securely attached or fastened, as any slippage on the move can affect stability and cause an unexpected accident. If you are using soft bags, you can use secure straps or bungee cords designed for motorcycles.

- **Test the Load:** After packing, taking your motorcycle for a short ride around your location with all equipment attached will help you check for any shifting in weight and make extra adjustments if necessary.

  Packing Tip: If you are using a top box, try to put basic or lighter items in there for easy access rather than overloading it as this can raise your motorcycle's centre of gravity.

12.5.5 ESSENTIAL PACKING TIPS AND SUGGESTIONS

In this section, I will try to give a few additional tips that can make a big difference on the road:

1. **Roll, Don't Fold:** Rolling your clothes instead of folding them saves space and keeps your gear more compact. You can also use vacuum bags to compress the clothes more, especially for longer tours.

2. **Plan for Multi-Purpose:** Trying to prefer some of the products you will take with you that have more than one function will help you reach more item capability with less items such as neck tubes and rain gear.

3. **Dry-Bag Electronics and Documents:** Always store electronic devices and important documents in waterproof bags for additional protection against unexpected rain, even if they are in hard luggage.

4. **Prioritise Accessibility:** Try to put items you will need frequently, such as snacks, water or raincoat, in an easily accessible place such as the top box.

Code: 114357

Additional Tip: It is very important to make a packing checklist when preparing for each trip so that you don't forget anything necessary behind. You can download the checklist I have prepared for you as a simple start by using the QR code on the side. This list will help ensure that nothing important is left behind and will also help you refine your packing over time, identifying items that are useful and items that can be left out.

Touring on a motorcycle is one of the most exciting experiences you can have, but without careful preparation and planning, a tour can be quite frustrating. In this chapter, I have tried to provide information on many different topics, from the right equipment, route planning, to the needs of international tours. I hope that this information will be a resource that will make your life easier on your tours.

13. THE COMMUNITY OF UK MOTORCYCLISTS

It would not be wrong to say that motorcycle riding is not only about riding, but also about a motorcyclist culture and community. Even greetings with other motorcyclists while riding your motorcycle in the UK will make you feel that you are accepted into this community without preconditions. Whether you are an experienced or beginner rider in the UK, you may need to reach out to a motorcycling community that will support you in various matters such as getting advice on a motorcycle-related issue, getting help and even finding a riding mate. In this chapter, I will explore how to connect with other motorcyclists through clubs, events, charity rides and online platforms.

13.1 MOTORCYCLE CLUBS AND SOCIAL GROUPS

Joining a motorcycle club or social group is not only an opportunity to ride with others but also a way to be part of a wider community that shares a passion for motorcycling. There are many clubs in the UK catering for a variety of interests and styles, from casual weekend rides to long distance touring or more advanced enthusiasts focussing on skill development. Group rides, meet-ups and events are the most common methods used by these societies. However, they can also come together to offer members the chance to gain new experiences, improve their riding skills and even support charitable causes.

13.1.1 FINDING LOCAL CLUBS

While in the past we used word of mouth to find local clubs, nowadays it is easier than ever to find a club in the area where you live or want to live, thanks to online and location technologies, it is easier than ever to find a club that suits your interests and experience level:

- **Local Motorcycle Shops:** Many motorcycle shops are trying to contribute to the community in the UK by serving as community centres. They may also support or partner with local clubs. Some shops may organise ride days, workshops and charity events, giving you the opportunity to learn about clubs in your area and meet other riders.

- **Online Platforms, Directories and Publications:** You can easily find motorcycle clubs through forums and social media platforms such as **Facebook** or **Meet-up**, which cater for both large clubs and smaller, niche riding groups across the UK. Another UK-specific resource is **The Biker Guide** website, which endeavours to provide comprehensive regional guides on many topics. In addition, **Motorcycle News (MCN)**, which is published weekly, shares motorcycle events from various parts of the UK every week, you can reach other motorcycle users with events in your area by viewing these sections.

- **Community Centres and Local Pubs:** Some clubs, especially in rural areas or smaller towns, hold regular meetings in community centres, pubs or cafes. Checking local notice boards and community centres is another way to find a club near you.

Tip: Although it varies according to the structure of the clubs, many clubs will allow you to attend a few rides or meetings as a guest before you become a member. This will be valuable as it will give you a chance to see if the group dynamics, riding style and activities suit your preferences. Apart from that, in some online clubs, free participation and prerequisites may not be required.

13.1.2 POPULAR MOTORCYCLE CLUBS AND GROUPS IN THE UK

There are a large number of motorcycle clubs in the UK catering for a variety of interests, riding styles and experience levels. It is of course not possible to list them all here, but I would like to share some of the active recognised clubs:

- **London Motorcycle Riders Club (LMRC):** With over 1,000 members, the LMRC is one of the largest motorcycle groups in London. The club constantly organises rides throughout the year, ranging from relaxed city rides to day tours out of the city. LMRC welcomes riders of all levels, including L-plate riders, to its rides and strives to provide a supportive environment for skill development and socialising.

- **The Institute of Advanced Motorists (IAM):** This club is more than just a club, as it also offers certification for those who wish to focus on riding skills and safety. IAM members can take advanced training courses, improving both their safety awareness and riding precision. This club will make it easier for you to connect with like-minded people who are committed to safe riding and will also help you improve your skills.

- **The Vintage Motor Cycle Club (VMCC):** For classic and vintage motorcycle enthusiasts, the VMCC, this club in the UK organises rallies, shows and group rides celebrating vintage motorcycles. The club has been operating since 1946 and can be a good choice for collectors and riders interested in historic machines.

- **The British Motorcyclists Federation (BMF):** One of the largest motorcycle organisations in the UK, the BMF represents the political, legal and safety interests of riders and offers a range of benefits to BMF members, including discounts on gear and insurance.

- **Harley Owners Group (HOG):** Harley-Davidson owners are part of a global club with local branches across the UK. HOG is a group that aims to create a strong sense of brand loyalty and community by offering its members opportunities to participate in special rides, rallies and social gatherings specifically for Harley riders.

Tip: Each club has a different style, some clubs focus more on social and recreational activities, others on safety, skills and community service. When choosing a club or group, consider your riding goals and interests and try to find the club that best suits you and your aspirations. You can find a lot of interesting club and groups via searching online.

13.1.3 GROUP RIDES AND MEET UPS

Group rides and meet-ups are one of the most common activities of many motorcycle clubs. These rides offer members the opportunity to explore new routes, learn from experienced riders and make friends.

- **Organised Group Rides:** Most clubs offer organised rides that can range from short local routes during the day to multi-day tours. Group rides usually follow a planned route, travelling with a designated ride leader and, where appropriate, a sweeper rider at the end of the group to ensure that the group does not break up. These rides are especially useful for new riders to learn group riding etiquette and help them gain experience on different types of roads.

- **Meet-up Events:** As well as rides, many clubs organise regular get-togethers at local cafes, pubs or community spaces where members can socialise, discuss motorcycle-related topics and plan future rides. Gatherings vary according to the goals and style of the club, but can sometimes include educational elements, including presentations on motorcycle maintenance, riding skills and trip planning.

- **Charity Rides and Fundraising Events:** Many clubs and associations organise charity rides to support causes ranging from veterans to health research. These rides provide participants with a sense of purpose and are important activities that contribute to building a positive image of motorcycling in the wider community.

Tips for Group Rides:

- **Pre-Ride Briefing:** In many group rides, the route is shared in advance, but it is still important to attend and participate in a pre-ride briefing just before the ride to explain the route, information for the weather related changes, planned stops, and rules for the group to ensure that your group ride is productive.

- **Ride at Your Own Pace:** It is important that you ride at a pace that you are comfortable with for general rides, except for rides that require some special skills. Do not put pressure on yourself to catch up with faster riders in the group. Most groups wait at designated points and often use a 'sweeper' method with a recovery rider from behind to ensure that no one is left behind.

- **Communication:** Use hand signals and check your mirrors regularly to be aware of other riders in the group and remember to apply the life-saving look, especially when overtaking.

13.2 MOTORCYCLING EVENTS IN THE UK

The UK hosts an impressive range of motorcycle events throughout the year, catering for all styles, from the casual weekend rider to the dedicated motorcycle enthusiast. You can attend many different events, from large annual gatherings where you can interact with the motorcycling community, witness skills demonstrations and discover the latest motorcycles, equipment and accessories, to more intimate niche rallies for specific brands or types of motorcycles.

13.2.1 MAJOR ANNUAL EVENTS

Throughout the year, you can take part in some of the most iconic motorcycle events in the UK, attracting motorcycle enthusiasts from around the world.

- **The Isle of Man TT:** Considered by many to be the most prestigious motorcycle race in the world, the Isle of Man is not part of the UK, but due to its location, it is one of the most important events to be mentioned here. Every year thousands of motorcycle fans come to the race, held in May and June, to watch the racers struggle at astonishing speeds on the winding mountain roads of the Isle of Man. The Isle of Man TT is a must-see event if you're looking for a challenging 37.73-mile round-trip through narrow bends and country lanes.

- **The MCN Festival of Motorcycling:** Organised annually by Motorcycle News (MCN) at the East of England Arena in Peterborough, the MCN Motorcycle Festival is one of the UK's most comprehensive motorcycle festivals. The festival offers live test rides, stunt shows, motorcycle demonstrations and camping options in a large area with major brands, making it a social weekend for participants who want to fully immerse themselves in the scene.

- **The Ace Café Reunion:** Celebrating London's historic Ace Café and café racer culture, this iconic event brings together motorcyclists from across the UK and Europe every September. Ace Café Reunion usually includes the Ace Café London to Brighton Burn Up ride as a weekend event, live music and motorcycle shows celebrating the café racer era. Attendees of all makes and models enjoy this event, although it's a great gathering for fans of classic motorcycles, vintage culture and custom builds.

- **The Motorcycle Live Show:** Held every November at the NEC in Birmingham, Motorcycle Live is the UK's largest motorcycle exhibition. Showcasing the latest models, equipment and accessories from top manufacturers, event also offers test rides, interactive demonstrations, stunt shows and workshops, allowing attendees to try new motorcycles, see the latest technology and learn from industry experts.

- **The Bike Shed Show:** Held in London's historic Tobacco Dock, The Bike Shed Show is a festival-like event that celebrates custom motorcycle culture by showcasing beautifully crafted motorcycles from manufacturers around the world. Known for its creative, relaxed vibe, the show features custom motorcycles, art exhibitions, food stalls, live music and lifestyle accessories. A must-visit event for café racers, scramblers, bobbers and all custom motorcycle enthusiasts.

Tip: It is wise to book accommodation and tickets in advance, especially as interest in the Isle of Man TT is very high.

13.2.2 NICHE AND LOCAL RALLIES

The UK is home to a variety of niche and local rallies catering for specific motorcycle types, brands and passionate regional communities. These events often offer different experiences and create strong bonds between smaller groups of enthusiasts.

- **Dragon Rally:** The Dragon Rally is one of the UK's most iconic winter events, taking place every February in harsh winter conditions despite the natural beauty of North Wales. The event sees participants camp overnight in freezing conditions to experience the true meaning and need for endurance and camaraderie. It is a truly satisfying challenge for riders who love the adventurous side of motorcycling and want to feel the sense of pride that comes with completing a rally.

- **The Welsh National Road Rally:** This navigation-based event aims to take riders around the breathtaking landscapes of Wales by setting their own route to visit a series of checkpoints. This event, where navigation skills are used, is an ideal event especially for those who enjoy touring.

- **Local Triumph and BMW Meetings:** Events such as BMW Motorrad Days and Triumph Tridays have their roots abroad, but UK enthusiasts often organise smaller scale meet-ups and rides. These informal gatherings are a useful way of building brand loyalty and increasing communication within the brand community.

13.2.3 POPULAR CHARITY RIDES

- **The Distinguished Gentleman's Ride:** The Distinguished Gentleman's Ride is an annual event that takes place in May each year and is well-attended across the UK, but is in fact a global event, combining style and social causes. Riders take scenic routes on classic or custom-built motorcycles, dressed in vintage or stylish clothing, to raise money for men's health, particularly prostate cancer and mental health. The event usually ends with social gatherings that seek to blend sophistication with community spirit.

- **Ride to the Wall (RTTW):** Held annually in October, this event aims to honour fallen British service personnel at the National Memorial Arboretum in Staffordshire. Large numbers of motorcycle riders make the journey to the memorial where a memorial service is held.

- **Bike4Life Ride Out and Festival:** Held in April each year, this ride is an organisation supporting the Midlands Air Ambulance Charity, a vital service for emergency medical assistance. Riders start from

Meole Brace in Shrewsbury and journey to Weston Park in Shropshire where a festival with live music, stalls and food awaits.

- **Charity Toy Runs:** Every December, motorcyclists across the UK take part in toy run rides through towns and cities to deliver toys to children's hospitals, hospices and shelters. These festive rides are usually open to all motorcyclists and invite participants to decorate their motorcycles with holiday cheer to serve a good cause.

13.2.4 TIPS FOR ATTENDING UK MOTORCYCLE EVENTS

- **Book Early:** Accommodation and tickets for popular events such as the Isle of Man TT can sell out quickly, so try to book in advance, this will not only secure your place but also provide an economic advantage.

- **Prepare for Weather:** Bring waterproof clothing as the UK weather can be unpredictable, even in summer.

- **Necessary Event Equipment and Clothing Requirements:** Before attending a specific niche or local rally, you should make sure you are well prepared by checking for specific event requirements, such as necessary equipment or gear.

- **Bring Essentials:** For longer events, especially rallies, remember to pack essential items such as a first aid kit, extra layers, and tools you may need for basic maintenance.

- **Engage with the Community:** Motorcycle events are a great place to network, share experiences and make lasting connections, so don't be afraid to start a conversation with other attendees. Starting this online in advance of the event will help you build a bond with attendees even before you attend the event.

13.3 ONLINE COMMUNITIES AND FORUMS

Recent technological advancements have made it simple for the expanding online motorcycle community to access a valuable resource: **online communities and forums**. These platforms are the ideal resource for both novice and expert riders because they include nearly everything a motorcycle enthusiast could ever need, including equipment reviews, mechanical guidance, route suggestions and trip stories.

For new riders, online forums can be an excellent way to ask questions and learn, open 24 hours a day, while experienced riders can get information about the problems and situations they experience according to their needs, share what they know with other riders, and even plan group rides with like-minded people.

13.3.1 POPULAR UK MOTORCYCLE FORUMS

Dedicated motorcycle forums make it easy for riders to find real-world information on a variety of topics such as safety, maintenance, riding techniques, event planning and even provide a space for in-depth discussions with other forum users, thanks to the correspondence they have accumulated over the years.

Although not as popular as they once were due to the more interactive nature of social platforms in recent times, forums are still active and are still valuable as a source of information. Some of the forums that are still active:

- **BikeChat Forums (BCF):** This forum offers sub-forums specifically for UK riders on topics ranging from learner tips to experienced rider advice. A dedicated "New Riders" section provides a wealth of content for beginners on the basics of licensing, insurance and equipment.

- **Adventure Bike Rider (ABR):** An active online forum for adventure motorcycle enthusiasts and readers of Adventure Bike Rider magazine. With thousands of members and hundreds of thousands of posts, it is a must-visit forum for discussions about magazine content, competitions and shared experiences.

Tip: Many forums have classified sections where users can buy and sell used motorcycle equipment and parts. If you need these types of second-hand parts, it can be a good place to look.

13.3.2 SOCIAL MEDIA GROUPS

Social media has become an indispensable part of the motorcycle community, especially in recent times. Platforms such as Facebook, Reddit and Instagram help motorcycle enthusiasts access a wide range of communities, with numerous groups and pages dedicated to different riding styles, motorcycle brands and local groups. These groups are often more dynamic than forums, with real-time text and visual updates and sometimes instantaneous communication speed, making them very attractive to users.

- **Facebook Groups:** Facebook is perhaps the largest medium in recent times to host a wide variety of motorcycle groups. Some groups focus on specific motorcycle brands (e.g. 'Honda Owners Club UK' or 'BMW GS Owners'), while others can provide regional diversity, such as 'London Bikers' or 'Scotland Bikers'.

There are also groups dedicated to riding styles, such as 'UK Adventure Riders' for adventure and off-road enthusiasts or 'Classic Motorcycles UK' for fans of vintage motorcycles. Facebook groups are a particularly suitable platform for organising meet-ups, posting invitations to ride or route information, and are widely used for these purposes in the UK.

- **Reddit:** The **r/motorcycles** subreddit is a large and active community where motorcycle riders regularly share trip reports, maintenance tips and equipment recommendations. For UK-specific discussions, check out **r/MotoUK**, where you'll often find pinned posts and FAQs in the subreddits, as well as some very useful discussions, especially if you're a beginner.

- **Instagram:** While it's not a discussion forum or a platform that brings together a community in a group mentality, Instagram is a popular platform for sharing photos of trips, custom motorcycle and equipment setups.

- **Meetup.com:** Meetup.com is a general social networking platform where various motorcycle groups across the UK share meet-up events. This platform is particularly suitable for meeting like-minded motorcycle enthusiasts face-to-face or joining group rides.

Tip: Every online community usually has some guidelines and rules to keep discussions productive and respectful. Always check the group rules before making a post. Some groups, especially on Facebook, may have certain restrictions on advertising, promoting events or posting about certain topics.

13.3.3 BENEFITS OF ONLINE COMMUNITIES AND FORUMS

- **Advice and Tips:** Whether you have a specific maintenance question or a request for route suggestions, online communities are invaluable as they bring together many people with many experiences. Experienced riders also learn from them, so they are happy to share their knowledge and help beginners.

- **Planning Group Rides:** If you are new to motorcycling, group rides are a great way to gain confidence and explore new routes with others. Many forums and social media groups organise regular rides and you can follow them and get involved in group rides.

- **Access to Exclusive Events:** Some online groups can plan special gatherings, charity rides, and training days for their members. You have the opportunity to take part in these activities and receive timely information because of these platforms.

- **Used Gear and Motorcycle Sales:** With many forums and groups having classified sections where members can buy or sell used motorcycles, equipment and accessories, these areas can be an alternative way of finding quality equipment to fit your budget.

- **Real-Time Updates:** Social media groups on Facebook are a good platform for this type of organisation to communicate, as they can provide real-time notifications of changes or updates to riding plans.

Final Note: Online communities can provide invaluable support and information, but especially when it comes to road laws, insurance or maintenance, it is important to remember to verify any technical or legal advice with the correct sources because these are their own opinion and interpretation.

13.4 APPS AND PLATFORMS FOR MOTORCYCLISTS

Motorcycle riders can now use various applications on their smartphones to improve their riding experience, such as traffic conditions, weather updates and navigation. Here I've tried to round up some of the most popular and useful apps among UK riders.

13.4.1 POPULAR APPS IN THE UK

- **MyRouteApp:** MyRouteApp is a comprehensive route planning application designed especially for motorcyclists, allowing users to create and share custom routes, as well as a web-based platform with detailed map layers and many route features. MyRouteApp also has the ability to export routes for many GPS devices, including TomTom and Garmin. The app also allows offline access, which can help you use seamless navigation even in areas with poor network coverage.

- **Calimoto:** Designed specifically for motorcyclists, Calimoto uses an algorithm to suggest winding and scenic roads, avoiding motorways as much as possible. Calimoto is a popular app for those who want to discover new riding routes and with options to save routes and share them with friends.

- **Scenic:** Scenic is a comprehensive navigation app created especially for motorcyclists, allowing riders to find, save and share routes with a user-friendly design for long-distance touring or weekend rides. The app also offers offline GPS functionality in remote areas with poor signal coverage.

- **MyRide:** Developed by Yamaha, MyRide is an application designed to track riding statistics and provide insights into performance data. Although developed by Yamaha, non-Yamaha riders can also use MyRide to monitor parameters such as distance, speed and elevation.

- **Detecht:** This app combines GPS navigation with safety features such as collision detection, emergency communication notifications and ride tracking. Detecht is designed for motorcycle riders and provides data on riding performance, helping you review speed, braking and cornering after every ride.

- **Waze:** A popular, community-driven navigation app that is also actively used by car users, Waze provides real-time traffic updates, road hazard warnings and speed camera notifications. For motorcyclists, Waze's live traffic data is useful for avoiding congestion and finding the fastest routes in busy city areas. It also allows you to set custom alerts for incidents, road closures and even fuel prices. Waze is especially popular for commuters or riders in urban areas looking for quick route adjustments on the go.

- **PetrolPrices:** Finding the cheapest fuel for long journeys can be difficult, especially in remote areas. Regularly updated to provide reliable data from across the UK, the app is particularly useful for drivers/riders travelling long distances looking to save on fuel costs.

- **Relive:** Relive is a GPS app that records your journey and creates a 3D video of your route, overlaid with photos, statistics and highlights from your journey. This app is popular with tour riders who want to visually capture and share their experience.

13.4.2 TIPS FOR CHOOSING THE RIGHT APPS

- **Test in Advance:** Before embarking on a big journey, test new apps to make sure they meet your needs and are compatible with your phone, and if it's a navigation app, it's worth testing it on your motorcycle. Each application has its own interface and being familiar with this interface will save you time and prevent you from having problems on the road.

- **Check Offline Capabilities:** Some apps offer an offline navigation feature, which is a must for riding in remote areas with limited phone reception, and especially if you are a motorcycle tourer, you should definitely consider this feature when choosing an app.

- **Stay Updated on App Features:** Many motorcycle apps regularly release new features and updates based on user feedback, so make sure you install these updates, especially some time before you go for a ride. But remember that some major releases can make big differences in usage and user interface visuals, and you should be sure to test to get used to the latest version.

- **Battery Management:** Especially running GPS-based apps and running multiple apps can quickly drain your phone's battery, so you may want to consider getting a portable charger, or a USB charger if your motorcycle doesn't have one, to ensure your devices stay on throughout the ride.

Whilst the list of clubs, events and online platforms in this section is by no means exhaustive, you can easily find countless other opportunities to get involved in the UK motorcycling community through your online research. As your motorcycling and your style evolves, trust that you will easily find the community that suits you.

Printed in Great Britain
by Amazon

56693526R00145